The Sacred
Portable Now

The Sacred Portable Now

The Transforming Gift of Living in the Moment

Daniel Singer
and
Marcella Bakur Weiner

PRIMA PUBLISHING

PRIMA PUBLISHING and colophon are registered trademarks of Prima Communications, Inc.

Library of Congress Cataloging-in-Publication Data
Singer, Daniel, 1949–
    The sacred portable now: the transforming gift of living in the moment /
    Daniel Singer and Marcella Bakur Weiner.
        p.   cm.
    ISBN 0-7615-0728-0
    1. Spiritual life.   I. Weiner, Marcella Bakur, 1925– . II. Title.
BL624.S5344   1996
291.4′4—dc20   96-32440
                                                                                     CIP

96 97 98 99 00 01 AA 10 9 8 7 6 5 4 3 2 1
Printed in the United States of America

How to Order
Single copies may be ordered from Prima Publishing, P.O. Box 1260BK, Rocklin, CA 95677; telephone (916) 632-4400. Quantity discounts are also available. On your letterhead, include information concerning the intended use of the books and the number of books you wish to purchase.

Visit us online at http://www.primapublishing.com

To my parents for the gift of life.
—Daniel Singer

For my brother, John Sol, who is always there in my eternal "now."
—Marcella Bakur Weiner

CONTENTS

CHAPTER THREE
The Heart of the Matter   31

CHAPTER FOUR
Minding Our Mind   43

CHAPTER FIVE
Dreams, Couriers of the Divine   59

CHAPTER SIX

The Body As Knowledge   77

CHAPTER SEVEN

The Messages of the Moment   95

CONCLUSION

The Colors of Life   107

ACKNOWLEDGMENTS

Georgia Hughes, our editor, has our deepest gratitude for her superb and caring work on behalf of this book. We thank our agent, James Levine, for his vision, faith, and expertise. We extend appreciation and thanks to Byron Eslava and Esther Makowsky for their invaluable technical support.

We wish to especially thank and acknowledge Dr. Gerald Epstein for his unique, creative, and generous contribution to our understanding of spirit and imagery.

We wish to extend our heartfelt love and appreciation to Will, Marcella's husband, for his infinite patience and sensitive feedback in the creation of this manuscript.

To all our clients and students, from whom we learn everything, we offer our profound thanks.

Daniel Singer wishes to acknowledge the contribution of the late Louise March to his own journey; and F. M. Alexander, Shlomo Carlebach and Robert Sigman, whose spirits all had an influence on the creation of this book. May their memories be eternally blessed. He is inexpressibly grateful to his dear friend, Patricia Masters, who predicted and encouraged this book from the beginning.

Introduction

❧

THE OCEANIC WISH

We condition ourselves to believe that life is finite, that it begins and that it ends. Immersed in the drama of our daily life, weighted with the demanding responsibility of our portion of Creation, we are profoundly absorbed in time and space. It is rare for the majority of us to find room in our busy existence for a connection to the limitless presence residing within the immediate moment. Riding the impermanent waves of action and reaction, we alternately submerge then float in a tide of spiritual forgetting and recollection.

The life that we are—each one a story of color, feeling, movement and sound—is rich with detail and nuance. These are the unique patterns of our personal mosaic, the singularity of form, belief and experience that we have come to call our humanness. Our particular stories interact with the stories of others, in gradations of intimacy, linking life to life, revealing one unified, global condition. None of us exists outside of or off the total grid.

Due to the ecological emergency we are reluctantly beginning to face, more of us are starting to regain the belief that everything is interconnected. Experience is rudely forcing us to wake up. The crisis of planetary survival is a tangible reflection that one part of the universe (that is, the human) needs to respect the whole, or there will be consequences to pay, including the possibility of extinction. It has already happened to certain parts of life on Earth. The web of interdependence is undeniable, and our nature is calling upon us to respond. Creation gives rise to everything life encompasses, whether it be the miracle of a fertilized ovum, an idea, an invention, or a rainy afternoon, the totality is greater than our vision. The miracle of the boundless is too awesome to hold and measure with the written word.

We have been given important gifts to help engender a spiritual connection in daily living. These are the gifts of appreciation and gratitude. The gift of appreciation is a catalyst for moving us into a condition of gratitude, one of the most potent seats of human possibility. Appreciation and gratitude are part of the spiritual and religious impulse, leading us toward a healthy humility and an active participation in our lives. Gratitude can help us to regain spirit, magnanimity of view, being and action. Appreciation and gratitude begin in the immediacy of the "now," where the present and the limitless connect. When we live in the past or the future, we miss this present moment, separating ourselves from our deepest spiritual possibility. We are an aspect of a oneness. A wave in the sea has a measurable height, volume, and life span, yet it is no less the ocean. Though we have a name, height, weight, and a particular life, we are not separate from the whole of the universe; and to be human is to live in alignment with the totality.

This book is an attempt to give practical hints and pointers, intended to remind us that we can indeed live the sacred impulse during ordinary day-to-day existence. There is no formula offered, no closed system. We take no position regarding the religious, spiritual and philosophical beliefs held by the reader. Our task here is to inform and remind the reader with an eye on the moment. A practical offering, we have left aside suggestions that would require finding a special time in the day or withdrawing from the world of activity. Quiet time and retreating are good and often necessary components of a spiritual "diet," but we tend to undervalue the opportunities abounding in the moment where we find ourselves now. This book presents means to approach a way of living that is more focused in the here and now. We believe that any positive effort toward spirit is a wonderful thing, and we place our emphasis on spiritual work within daily routines of living.

The challenge we face as modern people is living difficult, busy, distracted lives often separated from the experience of the spiritual dimension. Distanced from the spiritual present, one may experience a gnawing sense of meaninglessness or a persistent dryness of feeling. Often we daydream of a monastic experience, a quiet week on a desolate beach or a cabin-in-the-woods opportunity to turn inward, free of distraction. Whether the culprit appears to be the relentless needs of parenting, work, relationships, or just urban noise, we await the coming of a meditation class, a spiritual inspiration, available free time, one quiet hour or some other respite from the grind. In the meantime, life proceeds and little if any of our yearning is met in any tangible way.

The authors do not presume to inform readers of anything previously unheard of, or to present any kind of "superior techniques." The point is simply that there is no remedy but living more consciously in each moment we find ourselves in. If we imagine there is something "spiritual" that we need to do "in the future," in some other location, in order to engage our wish to be more present, then we deny the accessibility of the living present and substitute a future "tomorrow"—today being yesterday's "tomorrow"—ad infinitum, and never really begin. In this way we obviate the here and now. We might believe that the life we are living is somehow the obstacle separating us from a spiritual life. In some cases this might be a reasonable conclusion, based on the evidence at hand. But more often than not, it is our lack of perspective on what we have been given that is the foil. Even if we were residing in a spiritually supportive environment, it is still a set of circumstances. Wherever we are, we're called to accept the moment we are in. The tools necessary to negotiate a spiritually fulfilling experience of living a full and active life are often not sufficiently identifiable, let alone understood. One's taste of the various suggestions in this book can provide clarity for each person to see what is true for himself. Some will relate more to one chapter than to another. This is natural, for it is in conformity with the varieties of human type and predilection that one shoe does not fit all people. Nevertheless, no matter how we cut it, we are compelled by immutable laws of existence to begin wherever we may be.

Chapter 1

THE BIRD IN OUR HAND

You stub your toe. For a second, painful though it may be, you are in the moment. You are riding in your car when suddenly, without warning, a panorama of enormous and compelling beauty appears around the bend, taking your breath away. For a second, you are living in the moment. It is dusk. You are sitting, watching and listening to the ebbing tide of the ocean. Suddenly, for a moment, it is as if time stands still. That's living in the moment, the eternal, the present or the "now."

All experience of oneness with the universe—creation, a Creator, illumination, the eternal, spiritual work, meditation, prayer, gratitude, love, charity, and clarity—begins within the present moment. The doorway to spiritual growth, connection and contribution opens neither in the past nor in the future. It opens only in the presence of the present, the seat of the sacred, the "now."

Some rare people have experienced the fullness of living life completely and consistently in the fullness of the present, and others have intellectually acknowledged the value of discovering the sacred through the ever-present moment we find ourselves in. Many have had glimpses, rare moments that penetrate inner barriers to reach the spirit, opening a small crack, enlarging a wish. There are thousands of pages in philosophical, religious, and spiritual literature that address this truth.

As humans, we are related to time, conscious of the sunrises and sunsets, wearing watches, celebrating birthdays and creating schedules. The intention, action, experience and sacredness of life is met in the place of this moment, where we find ourselves, now. Timelessness is met in the present time. This is a universally acknowledged truth, remaining undisputed by any spiritual text, teacher, or source of which we are aware.

Of course, believing something to be true is one thing, but living it is something else. There is a marvelous expression being used these days: "Walk the talk." Our spiritual challenge, then, is to learn how to walk the talk. In other words, the talk may be expressed: "I want to live in the eternal present," or "The present moment is the deepest place to live one's life." The walk is to actually live presently in the sacred moment of the "now," sincerely and honestly taking the necessary steps to live that way, to walk the talk.

It's been a busy, hectic morning. Your lunch hour barely allows for enough time to visit the bank and use the cash machine. Eagerly, you arrive only to find a line of eleven people ahead of you. Forced into the disquieting situation of a long wait, you fidget and fuss. Staring with anticipation and some annoyance at the people on line, you furtively look for another person with whom you can commiserate and share your frustration. You nervously drum your fingers on your briefcase, then check inside for some item that you already know is there. Thoughts are racing about all sorts of irrelevant imaginings, past and future scenarios arising and overheating the mind. Gradually you become annoyed at your coworker, the one who had suggested the lunch time for going to the bank. Then you start to worry about something you remember you must do back at the office, and the potentially sluggish traffic situation after work. You move on into worrying if it is going to rain on the weekend.

Is there any possibility of living in a sacred moment in this kind of state? Some elusive part of you knows that you are capable of significantly more than this, but you're stuck. Or are you?

We are specialists at living in fragments. Living in the past and living in the future are very easy to do. The joys and sorrows of the near and distant past are replayed through recollection and repetition, and the future is rehearsed through anticipation. We seem bound by the constraints of what was and what (we expect) will be. To reverse this predicament, to fulfill the spiritual promise that is the privilege of life, requires practical tools, inner methods, and above all, effort. With clear method and sincere effort we can shift our perspective to encompass the sacredness of being purposefully in the moment.

Witnessing

Back at the bank, waiting in line, let us create a different scenario, one more consistent with spiritual growth. While waiting in line, you make a serious, conscious effort to notice your reactions and accept them as your own creation, informed by the past and fed by the future. When trapped, we often need a little distance, a bit of maneuvering space. Through this action of witnessing, noticing the irritation and frustration for what it is, your wits have been partially spared. You haven't lost your wits entirely, or else you would not be able to consciously notice your entanglement in this situation. (Interestingly, *wits* and *witness* have the same Old English root, *witan,* "to know.")

By this simple act of witnessing, you have moved somewhat into the present, having met some limited sanity within your habitual, seemingly out-of-control reactions. You then make a shift into awareness of your physical body. Again, you have moved back into the moment. Sensing tension in the knees, you let them ease and soften, allowing the arches of your feet to clearly support the weight of the body, like a tree well rooted in the ground. Arms and hands hanging by the side, you relax the palms and fingers while gently, imperceptibly, rocking over the ankles until you sense a new, mobile stability, more balanced, more poised. Again, you have moved into the present. Doing these little things quietly, unobtrusively, free of any drama, nobody else is even noticing us doing this. It is your private contribution to a moment of sanity in the world, our internal work, a personal intentional effort, a sacred treasure. Experiencing the breath, the torso expanding and contracting, you feel the rhythms of your respiration going in, then out. Now giving up tension in the fore-head, the tongue and the lips, your face relaxes. You create an "inner smile," a smile barely perceptible. It is not a forced social smile. It is small and not for anyone else but yourself. Mysteri-ously, now, there has been a shift in the inner state. Fewer unneeded thoughts and imaginings clutter the mind. Less anxious, more focused, the senses are less cloudy, more appre-ciated. Then we notice a mother with a baby in the infant stroller. We hadn't noticed them before. Such a beautiful baby, full of newness and interest in life! The person behind asks for the time. You converse and chuckle together over something or another. Much to your surprise, the unhappiness, the frustration has melted away and the annoyance you felt has evaporated. You are in the present. It is now your turn to use the cash machine. Where did the time go? You exit the bank. Outside the sun bathes the sidewalk. You no longer feel like rushing, so you walk, unhurried, back to the office, a deeper, more conscious side of living having revealed itself.

Today, more than at any other time in recorded history, we are awash with information, knowledge, wisdom, and guidance. We can drive to a lecture, watch a television program about con-cepts of living, fly to a great spiritual teacher 8,000 miles away; or plug into the Internet and access the writings of an ancient philosopher from Crete. Knowledge can encourage and inspire us. Of this there is little doubt. But, again, until we have lived and personally experienced what is being offered, it remains known but not understood, fed to us but not chewed and digested. As the saying goes, "You are what you eat." We need to consume, digest and become the wisdom we are served if we are to be nourished by it.

The Perseverance of the Present

Our desire to live in the present needs to be translated into some-thing more active than just a recurring wish. If we have the wish and we leave it unexamined, unexplored and never realized, we feed into a subtle spiritual hopelessness, a sense of isolation from the sacredness of life. Our spiritual potential becomes increas[ ] submerged in life's momentum and we lose precious time.

The present is always waiting to come into our experience, like a friend who is looking for us. The action we take to meet this friend is to prepare our home for her arrival. We have the power to act, to make ourselves ready in an active form of waiting. Again, if we try to find the present and go after it with greed, it will most likely navigate away from us. So any method needs our honesty and simplicity. Subtlety and an abiding sense of experimentation may be the most effective approach.

Imagine walking to the store and buying some sponges. We generally don't keep thinking, "I am walking to the store and I am buying sponges," like an insistent, never-ending mental chant. For once the goal has been set, the next step is to act out the process. In this case, we act to walk and then to buy the sponges. This is an essential principle. Shifting from the thought or intention to do something, we move the attention to the next step and act.

Shifting into the moment operates with the same principle. We choose to be more in the moment and then we move into the next step. The action we make is specific to our own way, our own choices, but it is action nevertheless. At times it is an inner action, other times, it is an inner and outer action in concert. But the shift is clear, real and identifiable to ourselves. By taking action in a certain way, we move into the present. While for some of us recall of the living moment does not provide a sufficiently complete understanding of the role of spirit in daily affairs, nevertheless, such attention is one of the most challenging and oft-neglected components of the spiritual path as applied to daily living, whether the teaching is Western or Eastern in origin.

We may miss being in the moment by trying the wrong way. Perhaps you have experienced trying too hard to befriend someone—at a party, for instance—only to have them move farther away from you. The whole effort may turn into a fiasco. You are "trying," yet you produce the opposite of your desire. Instead of befriending someone, you have created uncomfortable feelings, and maybe even enmity. To put it another way, sometimes when we are up at bat we try so hard to hit the ball correctly that we end up striking out from all the tension. Again, our "trying" has sent us farther from, rather than closer to, our original goal.

We need to become more skillful about being in the moment. One might argue that it's not the trying that is problematic, but rather how one tries. But how do I appropriately take the next step into action? What do I need to do to gain greater access to the present moment?

The Noticed Moment

One way is to start to notice oneself in life. Gentle self-observation is not very fancy. It need not be embellished as an elusive mystery. Familiar with observing a ship passing, or a setting sun, we also have the capacity to observe ourselves. We can observe emotions and feelings, physical sensations of the body, the five senses, and thoughts. These are sweeping categories, but they are loosely presented here to help us make certain distinctions, which can be very useful in fine-tuning our perception and honing our spiritual efforts.

Try this exercise. It will give you the experience of what we mean by *witnessing* or *observing*. Get up, go to a sink, and wash your hands thoroughly. Then return to where you were sitting, pick up this book and read on. Stop here and do the exercise.

Now ask yourself the following questions:
"Where were my thoughts when I was washing my hands?"
"What was I thinking? *Was* I thinking?"
"How did I feel while I was washing my hands?"
"What physical sensations did I experience when I washed my hands?"

Don't dwell on the answers. Just let them rise up in your awareness. If you have a clear answer to any of these questions, even if it is simply a one- or two-word answer, then you have witnessed or observed a thought, feeling, or sensation. If you came up with an answer like "I don't know," then you were probably not paying attention to that part of washing your hands. In that case, repeat the exercise and make a gentle effort to witness the sensation of the water running through your fingers as you wash your hands.

Feelings vs. Emotions

The words *feeling* and *emotion* are often assumed to have the same meaning. However, they are distinct words with distinct meanings. In casual conversation, most of us use these two words interchangeably, believing them to be synonymous. This can be limiting for our inner journey toward the present moment.

When we experience profound loss, through death or the parting of a relationship, there is a pain that appears that is universal and deep. Loss is a natural feeling, exquisitely pure, painful though it may be. Mourning is as natural as a rainy day, and it has its own appropriate duration. This is real and a necessary human response. Not meant to be ignored, pushed aside or denied in any way, its arising is spontaneous, involuntary. It is a way of the heart, coming and going in its own time, following an inner clock that knows how to heal us and allow us to proceed in life. Loss is a feeling.

There is another human response that is similar to, but quite different from, a feeling. This is called an emotion. It is a response that includes an extra element of the mind or recollection.

Let's go back and reexamine the scenario of waiting on line at the bank machine, experiencing annoyance and frustration. Here we are adding thoughts, stories, expectations, comparisons, and a wandering mind to the moment. With such an extra element, we create what we call an emotion. As real as a feeling, an emotion includes the past and the future. It can include a thought like, "The world is always against me," or "If so-and-so had not encouraged me to come to the bank, this would never happen." Or, "I expected going to the bank at lunch time would be a speedy affair," and so on. Emotion derives its often overwhelming power from something other than the present we are living in.

Understanding this distinction, by learning the difference between an emotional experience and a feeling experience, we are able to differentiate between living in the past, the future or living in the present. The past experience that drives an emotion may have been a real drama that did occur, or a belief we have had about ourselves or the world, but it exists now only as a script or a set of conditions with which we are meeting the phenomenal world. Thus we create something more complicated, a response not originating entirely from the clean-slate of the present. In fact, in some situations, we may find that we are experiencing a great deal of emotion and virtually no feeling. It is not a question of emotions being wrong and feelings being right, but it is useful to learn to distinguish between them for learning about living in the moment. We can notice that feelings reside in the heart and emotions take place in both the heart and the mind. Again, emotions are not worse or better than feelings, but they are distinct.

Imagine you are hammering a nail into a wall and the nail bends. Most of us mutter an expletive or our favorite curse. We are thinking, "This is a problem and problems cause discomfort and I remember what discomfort feels like because I've experienced it before." Our response is linked to thoughts, memories, and conclusions from the past. The sentiment, arising and being discharged by muttering an expletive, is an emotion, not a feeling. The feeling was actually surprise, a response to a change in circumstance, an unforeseen event of a nail bending. Surprise might have lasted but two seconds, and could have simply become a fact to be dealt with. The nail needs to be removed and replaced, requiring only presence and action in the moment.

Now imagine that you accidentally step on the tail of a dog whom you have befriended. The dog yelps, then growls at you once. He feels pain and violation. Then, in the next moment, he accepts your apology and you are friends again. The dog is demonstrating a feeling going through its paces. There is no emotion. There is no past, no memory. The dog is living completely in the experience, rooted and flexible in the moment.

As human beings, we are blessed with the gift of feeling. To feel deeply is to live deeply. Paradoxically, emotionality can displace true feeling. When we experience highly emotional states, we are experiencing feelings we had in the past regurgitating in the present through the vehicle of memory, creating emotion. We can also experience intensity of feeling, like pure joy or pure revulsion. The important thing to remember is that feelings are from the present and emotions are from expectation, extra thoughts, or the past.

A Perennial Perspective

We come into being as and with a consciousness. Some traditions name this presence "the witness." As we experience life and learn new things, the witness appears and submerges in the river of our existence. But it is always there. Depending upon our choices, the witness can become our servant or our master. It is our overall awareness. It is the seat of alertness. It watches over all the functions of the mind, the heart, and the body. It is the part of ourselves that experiences our life in its largest context.

When we are overwhelmed by the demands of life, the intensity of circumstances or desire, our attention usually shifts away from the witness and is pulled against the larger, spiritual context. This is the opposite of the awareness and attentiveness that serves the spiritual quest. The ability of outside events and desires to pull at and demand our energy never ceases in life. Despite the challenges of external demands, it is also this important function that grabs our attention in an emergency and allows us to make a quick and necessary response. Unfortunately, it is overworked and overused and therefore exhausts our ability to place our awareness where we wish, to respond attentively rather than simply react to life.

Intentional observation or witnessing is a form of cleansing. What it does is give a perspective to whatever occurs. Lighting up a deeper intelligence, it allows us to be just a little freer in life, less stuck in the events and our reactions to them. Witnessing allows us to stay inwardly mobile and available while still living in the world, whether the world brings us pleasure or discomfort.

The things that happen to us, the states that control us and the habits of thinking appear to go on endlessly. They are what we get stuck in. Through our lack of discernment we give them unnecessary power over our experience of living. Events "take over" and obscure our essential well-being. If we believe that circumstance determines our states, this must mean we feel controlled by life. We never really love what controls us inwardly. Therefore, we might never deeply love and cherish a demanding life as we were originally designed to do.

Without perspective, without a larger context and view of our experience of life, it is difficult to see how we can hope to experience the vast oneness of the universe, or something as enlightened as universal love or compassion. Without learning to have perspective, like the perspective which comes from some serious measure of witnessing, we are incomplete.

Life need not be filled with extra sorrow, unnecessary suffering above and beyond what is meant for our portion. We might fail to notice the paucity of illumination in our life until a shock wakes us up. We can also be spiritually asleep and believe we are wide awake, or, of equal misfortune, not even care one way or the other. We need not support the darkness. We can move toward the light by way of the moment.

"Living in the moment" is not to be confused with an irresponsible reactivity, which claims the mantle of "spontaneity" and wreaks havoc in one's own and other people's lives. Honestly living in the moment has no destructive component. If you are drunk and you decide to get behind the wheel of a car, this is an irresponsible and potentially destructive decision. It is the opposite of living in the moment. What is egotistical, selfish or endangering to life, be it one's own or another person's, derives from a lack of respect for the moment, a lack of consciousness about the present. It comes from our conditioning, our habitual tendencies which are not of the moment.

Morality, whether personal or collective, originates from a quality of consciousness, an intuitive or divinely inspired relationship to the "now." All the great teachings of the ages contain moral guidance which came through people who lived in the moment under specific social and cultural conditions.

The actions we can take to live in the moment are more about getting rid of something and opening to something, rather than about acquiring something new. What we seek is already here. There is something to be done, but the "doing" is a process of shifting perspective. It is subtle, small and simple. Different, yet also similar to how we ordinarily approach things, it can seem quite elusive. But our path into the moment can, in fact, be quite concrete, leading us into the living present. The portable "now" becomes more and more accessible within our experience.

The Action of Awareness

Using life as our workshop, any moment that presents itself can be acted upon by witnessing some aspect of ourselves. As we mentioned previously, it is possible to witness or observe our thoughts. I can think, "I want to buy some shoes." I can also notice *that I am thinking*. What is the significance of this shift?

When we have a thought of wanting something, we often become enslaved or entangled by that thought. We lack significant and sufficient awareness for the door to spirit to open. When we choose to observe a thought, we become more than the thought. We become (to some extent) the larger consciousness we seek, the awareness we dream of, the calm at the eye of the hurricane.

Witnessing is always the beginning for us. It is the first rung of the ladder that can lead us toward a view that can encompass the sacred. It starts with awareness of ourselves, the most immediate and always available reflection of the divine. We find the ordinary in life and there we begin.

You are using a vacuum cleaner. Your mind races, wandering from strategy to strategy, speculation to speculation. Like the fictional character Walter Mitty, all sorts of fantasies absorb your attention. You are mildly preoccupied with every passing thought. The vacuum cleaner is on automatic, and so are you. Everything is taking your attention except the vacuuming. If we could read each other's thoughts, we'd see how extraordinarily overwhelming and universal is the wandering mind. Witness the thoughts moving and passing, one after another, like a chattering flock of birds passing overhead. But as in a flock of birds, there are spaces where one thought has ended and another has not quite begun.

Witness the spaces between the thoughts. As you witness the spaces, you might notice them getting larger, or clusters of thoughts passing by less frequently. The thoughts are subsiding in their intensity and they distract you less from the task at hand. We become alive to the moment, open, able, happy, alert, and present to the necessary task of vacuuming the living room.

The beauty of witnessing is that we can notice not only thought, but the nuances of feeling, emotion, and sensation. Instead of losing ourselves in an emotion, we can find ourselves by witnessing. Becoming proficient at the skill of observation, we can also notice when there are spiritually opportune openings for greater appreciation and gratitude of what we are given. We can notice when our state becomes calm—and we can experience that calm. We can enter into the moment even more completely when we learn to notice, in a subtle and unobtrusive way, what is happening to our inner state. The vastness of a starry summer night in the country might then penetrate and transform us even more deeply.

The inner state we dwell in becomes our choice. It is not about control. It's about freedom from those things within ourselves that keep us from experiencing the sacredness of our journey. So much masks our spiritual inheritance, interfering with our taste of life and the appreciation of our existence.

It is said that a bird in the hand is worth two in the bush. Working with where we are, now, we can leave behind all the spiritual speculation and get down to business.

A daily life of activity, feelings, sensations, smells, colors and sounds, all rich in detail, is the spiritual challenge we are given. No matter what our spiritual belief or religious background may be, the moment we are in is the most logical place to start. We delay our journey by thinking there is another time and place when we will actually begin to engage in the spiritual side of existence. Beginning in the present tense, in this very moment, we start to make a connection to the sacredness of all of life, not merely the obvious high points and blessings that make us feel particularly happy. There is a deeper sense of presence and well-being which is the arena of spiritual activity, beyond the level of happiness and sadness. This is the level where access to spirit creates a flexible strength that carries us through our journey and enlightens life in all its colors. This sacred engagement of a moment in life is not dependent on circumstance, beautiful settings, or supportive environments. It depends only on us, where we each find ourselves and make efforts to deepen our existence in a moment. Much of life has repetition and predictability, but the larger task is to connect with our spiritual nature even when the circumstances appear quite ordinary, for life is our workshop and we are the artisans of the sacred.

Chapter 2

THE SACRED VALUE
OF PAYING ATTENTION

When we realize that we can have a living relationship with the attention we make a major leap into the moment and toward the divine. The attention is always available, waiting to be rediscovered and used for a larger good. It is mobile, flexible, stretchable, and highly accessible. For most of us it is rusty and we are unfamiliar with its ways and possibilities. As we get to know it and use it, the attention can become a strong, vibrant "home base." Like a muscle, the more it is used appropriately, the stronger it becomes.

In our daily life, our spiritual possibilities are connected to the strength, vitality, and mobility of our attention. Each one of us has unique life conditions and circumstances. Some of us are healthy, some are ill. Some are struggling with difficult family responsibilities and relationships, others with loneliness. Some experience financial security, others struggle to make ends meet. But the attention, like the heartbeat, is the continuous constant in our life.

It is nighttime. Alighting with unassuming poise, a spotted fawn conquers a country stone wall and stops, held fixed by the sudden appearance of the glaring headlights of an oncoming car. The deer responds instinctively to an unknown, a potential point of danger.

On a street in France, a crowd gathers, attracted by a street performer fiddling medieval music on an obscure and odd-looking instrument from antiquity.

In a suburban home in Minnesota, a grandfather sits on his sofa, slowly, carefully, lovingly unraveling a heavily knotted shoelace for his four-year-old grandchild.

Like the deer mesmerized by the headlights of a car, our attention is taken by compelling and sudden events. Like the crowd enraptured by the medieval music, our attention moves toward what interests us. And like the grandfather untying the shoelace, we are routinely called to place our attention on the needs that arise in the course of any given day.

Rarely appreciated, our inherent capacity to be attentive is the starting point, the elemental building block from which all spiritual activity begins. It is perhaps one of the most basic functions we have. We know we have eyes to see with, ears to hear with and a nose with which we smell. Yet, not often acknowledged in our upbringing and by our education and culture is another mysterious function. This function is the ability to be attentive.

A Sacred Sinew

Just as we have eyes, ears, and a nose, we seem to have some sort of unidentified "organ" to be attentive with. But this is really not as important as is the basic fact that we can be attentive to ourselves, others, and things.

All sacred components of our life are experienced by way of the wellspring of human attention. Negativity, feelings of despair, imbalance, lack of clarity, and stagnation of the spirit also are a byproducts of choices made by the very same attention. Part of the design of the attention allows it to be attracted to something or purposely placed on something. It can be weak, strong, deficient, adequate or extraordinary in meeting a demand. It functions almost like a muscle does. In fact, the root of the word *attention* comes from the Latin *attendere*, "to stretch to." (Perhaps that is why we say things like, "It was a stretch to follow what he was saying.")

The attention is given to us as a gift on loan. It is not ours because, from a spiritual perspective, we don't really *own* anything. We can only own that which cannot be taken from us. But like any gift on loan, we have the responsibility to use it with care and discretion, because it is our portion of the gift of life that we have received.

When we hand someone a bouquet of flowers, we use a certain set of muscles in our arm. By the same token we could use the same muscles to steal something or hit someone. It is not the muscle which is responsible for how it is used. The muscle is essentially innocent and at the service of the action we choose to perform with it. This is the human element of choice, consent and free will.

The choice of action and the responsibility for the action is ours. Unless severely impaired, the attention might also be understood as essentially neutral. It is flexible and willing to be used at the service of what is important to us in any given moment.

A typical toaster uses electricity to make your favorite bread warm, crispy and delicious in the morning. But this very same electricity can burn toast and make it unpalatable. Or it could even become dangerous should it short-circuit and start a fire in the kitchen. Whether to our advantage or disadvantage, attention, like electricity, is essentially neutral. What matters in our experience is where it goes, where it is directed, and how we use it.

When we are doing routine activities in life, like answering the phone, reacting to something someone says about us, buying groceries, or hanging up a coat, we most probably are using our attention in a way born of habit and repetition. These habitual routines of daily living might work well, but only to a certain degree. They are strategies, for better or for worse, that allow us to survive but not necessarily to thrive spiritually. They assist basic physical survival, but are not necessarily connected to the spiritual side of existence. But they need to be respected for the important role they play in our life. Our ordinary manner in the world is an important and necessary part of who we are. It is our starting point for "stretching" toward a richer relationship to the moment.

Self-condemnation and self-judgment are useless and damaging substitutes for a healthy examination of who we are. Learning to know ourselves is a time-tested method that respects the nature of who we are. Internal invective and self-deprecation are off the mark and can lead us far away from our original sacred impulse.

The Seed of Metamorphosis

The purpose of this chapter is to introduce the challenge of using the attention as the foundation of a sacred discipline in daily life. We have established the fact that life is largely a product of the attention. What we do with the attention is an important part of our quest. Why?

The greatest difficulty that people have in life is following through with inspiration. Stirring talks, fascinating concepts and brilliant expositions do not necessarily get us to "walk the talk." Something interferes with our earnest pursuit of a higher road. Most of us have unprecedented access to information on any subject we wish, yet we seem to lack a certain strength, a certain "stick-to-it-ness" that is necessary for developing attractive ideas into real practice.

Most of our actions are complicated by an unproductive array of unnecessary thoughts, ideas, anxieties, expectations, memories, and tensions that prevent us from being simple. Spirit is simple, but complications mask simplicity from our view. We barely notice how complicated we make things because we are usually inattentive or else our attention is so automatic that we are in a frenetic tizzy or a sleepy daze. With this quality of attention it is no wonder that we feel separated from a deeper, more spiritual side of ourselves. We have limited ourselves to automatic attention in most of what we do and life seems too complex. Inattentive to what is going on in our mind, our heart, our body, and our world, we dream and wish for higher understanding.

We might run around a lot, do a lot and worry a lot, but our level of connection to our experience usually falls far short of its real potential.

You are watching television. Absorbed in a very clever commercial that has cost hundreds of thousands of dollars to produce, you are glued to the set, taken in by image after image. Your attention has been called forth and seduced by what is taking place on the screen. This is where your attention is.

A good place to begin is to ask ourselves the question "Where is my attention?" There is no right or wrong here. There is no "should," as in, "My attention should be on the vegetables I am cutting." Rather, we are learning to be objectively watchful, getting to know where we are placing our energy, without harshness or expectation. We are befriending an aspect of ourselves that, up until now, has run mostly on its own steam. Like befriending a reluctant person, we have to watch, listen and act with care, receptivity and an open heart. We are forging a relationship with a part of ourselves that requires effort and compassion. It has been said that what is above is also below. The universe exists in correspondences. If we show compassion and effort toward ourselves, we will be able to have compassion and make efforts for others.

Pausing here for a moment, let's look at this in the larger context of the sacred. Experiencing greater sense of being centered, a divine vibrancy or a spiritually rewarding moment, means there has been some sort of internal shift. The wholeness of eternity, or the oneness of the universe—or whatever name you give it—hasn't changed, but you have gone through a metamorphosis, a change of some sort. Perhaps there is a moment of flowing simplicity, a moment in which you might feel more peaceful or more centered, a new presence of mind, or even a great religious feeling, sensing the existence of something greater than yourself. Or you simply might feel happier, more alive, more available to the task at hand.

Experiences of the sacred come with many qualities. There is no limit to that which is sacred because it comes from a limitless source. Each human being has unique ways of experiencing events. Everyone is an expression of the same oneness, but we will each experience this oneness in our own personal moment, our own individual style.

If you have chosen to read this book, something in you is no doubt interested in going beyond the chance encounter with the sacred impulse, toward a more intentional, frequent and consistent relationship to spiritual effort.

From Inertia to Intention

Chance encounters with spiritually rich moments are very real and important wake-up calls. They can remind us of our potential relationship to creation. However, barring the exceptional circumstance, they are invariably relegated to the "fond memory" bank, where they help us to sleep through our daily life more soundly.

Richard lives the hectic life of a corporate lawyer. Financially well off, he spends most of his life working fourteen-hour days and squeezing in "quality time" with his wife and two children. Driving down the highway, Richard has a near head-on accident with an oncoming car. Quick reflexes and a fast swerve to the right avert the accident, but Richard is shaken to the core. Recognizing the fragility and the preciousness of life, he returns home to spend the rest of the day with his wife and children. Sharing his experience with his wife, he tells her that he feels closer to God, more connected to what is most important. Not easily able to describe the feeling-sensation, he tells her that he feels more spiritual, more whole. The next day he speaks to his brother long-distance on the phone. His brother had at one time contemplated going to a seminary and was considered "the spiritual one in the family." Their talk is deep, moving, and loving. Richard feels his life is changing, but he knows not how. Seven months pass by and Richard and his brother are at a family wedding. Wondering how things developed for his brother since their intense conversation of the previous summer, the brother eventually inquires after Richard's previous resolve to read some books on prayer and meditation. A little embarrassed, Richard realizes that he had quickly returned to the mental state and priorities of his life before the near-accident. Things had just gotten lost in the muddle of a busy life. Spirit had revealed itself, and had quickly returned to its elusive hiding place. An opening was given but Richard didn't fully understand that he could have made important changes in his life, if he had had some tools.

We mostly sleep through our daily life unless we awaken the attention. Our need for connection with ourselves is the necessary prerequisite for connecting to the world and to others. The occasionally arising, unintended impulse to awaken to the divine requires that we build upon it and strengthen it. We seek an intentional opening to spirit. Only when we make intentional choices can our deepest spiritual yearnings be made real. This constancy of purpose and carry-through comes from the attention.

An Intelligent Shopper

Picture yourself pushing a shopping cart through a supermarket. You are intent on getting your shopping chores done. Let's look at this rather ordinary task respecting the attention and see how we can work with it.

When we decide to go shopping in the supermarket, we have a marvelous opportunity to exercise conscious, rather than unconscious, use of the attention. We need to make a conscious choice to return to the simplicity of being attentive for the sake of all that we value, in keeping with our spiritual aspirations. In the spiritual life we are always looking for a consistency and continuity of purpose that transcends circumstance and embraces everything presented to us in life.

In our day-to-day life, it is a common habit to fall prey to the ups and downs of external circumstances and the moods they apparently engender in us. Thoughts may run wild, emotions raise and lower our spirits, and the sensations of the body can run the gamut from exhilaration, disquietude, or dullness. The continuity of our day requires scheduling activities and following them through. It would appear that the spiritual life that percolates on a low flame within us must wait until there is a chance to find some quiet time, or further inspiration from a respected book or person. Alas, there appears to be no space for the spiritual side of life, on the inside or the outside. This is a mistaken view; for all traditions, great poets and spiritual paths acknowledge that ordinary life and the life of spirit are occurring simultaneously. It is our stagnation, our inability to act with a recollection of our spiritual nature that stands in the way of fuller appreciation of what a day in a life contains. By taking a common task such as shopping and making the decision to seek a different level of experience within this familiar and ordinary part of life, we return to our deeper strivings, our spiritual inclinations.

By this time in our life, most of us have developed the skills, the knowledge, the know-how to push a shopping cart through a supermarket and shop. It is an important skill. It feeds us and provides us with tools for sustaining our physical existence. On the animal level, it is a good and useful activity, necessary for acquiring what we need. On the outside, a supermarket certainly appears quite different from a house of prayer, a meditation center, a spiritual gathering, or a quiet moment in a room by oneself. On the surface, it is not particularly conducive to connecting to the spiritual life. It just is what it is, and serves well the function for which it was created.

Let's distinguish our habitual, ordinary, uninformed way of shopping from this proposed, more conscious way. Let's call it "active shopping." We'll call it that because the attention must become more active if we are to simplify and consciously embrace the moment.

Visualize a time when you or someone else acted forthrightly, with profound clarity, simplicity and interest. Perhaps it was in an emergency, perhaps not. The attention became very alive and active, and it cut through unnecessary thought, second-guessing, or unproductive emotions. And, by being active, it kept things correspondingly simple. Many people describe such moments as "time stood still," or, "I felt totally alive and in the present," or, "Fear left me and I felt at one with everything."

This idea of active shopping is presented as an example of a possible starting place for us to mobilize our attention in a more conscious and life-affirming direction. It is not the only place to begin, for in truth there are many ways to enter into a larger context, a deeper picture, a sacred effort. A suggestion of this sort is meant simply as an example, a pointer. It is absolutely not suggested as a chant or a mantra, but only as an idea to come back to when we choose to do something supportive for our spiritual life. It is a reminder, a first step in shifting the attention. Without a conscious beginning effort, whether refined or less subtle, the sacred life eludes us and lies fallow like a field not sowed. A seeker, however, turns the soil and plants. Making choices with the attention, we are active wherever and whenever we can, finding help along the way.

So here we are. Pushing a cart in a supermarket. We remember that we want to do something beneficial for the inner life. We can actually begin anywhere. For example, when we push a shopping cart we are given a wonderful opportunity to learn how to let go of unnecessary physical tension. On the average, we grip the handles of the shopping cart unconsciously, holding tightly, with all that implies. Grasping, holding on, fear, anxiety, all the haunting qualities that we are capable of are right there, in the way we grip the cart. All of these difficult qualities obstruct and cover over an abiding sense of the ineffable oneness. Yet, the difficult qualities we bring to our activities are excellent ways to get a handle on what interferes with a more peaceful, present and alive self, capable of experiencing the spiritual dimension within a moment. Therefore, when gripping the shopping cart, check to see just how much tension you truly need to push it. Not too little and not too much. Let's see how this is a useful practice.

First of all, by making the decision to tune into the level of tension in the hands, it takes us from the automatic, habitual way of being in any old state, into a new place within. It makes life in that moment more intentional, therefore more conscious. It is a simple turn toward an inner action that has no other purpose but to increase intention for the benefit of the spiritual life. It is like a quiet, personal microshift in consciousness, important because it is small and accessible. We have made a precise decision to seize the moment and strive for a more conscious relationship to one aspect of the "now."

Second, much of the tension in the body is reflected through tension in the extremities. By being aware of the unnecessary tension in the hands, we are also affecting the tension in the rest of the body. This is a demonstration of the principle that the part contains the whole. When we affect a small shift of focus in a part, we create a shift of focus in the whole. The elimination of unnecessary physical tension is a very common element in spiritual work. Ease becomes coupled with activity and choice to merge our receptivity with the details of the activity we are involved in. Openness to spirit can often start with a connection to the physical body, by giving our interest to sensation, some inquiry concerning balance, tension, or breath. It is important to note that we are speaking of releasing unnecessary tension in our hands, not about extreme relaxation. Life requires balanced tension, like an umbrella that is open. Appropriate tension, not too much, is balanced tension. Otherwise, by exaggerating the impulse to find deep relaxation, we go limp and lifeless, unable to function well.

Third, when we ground our attention in a simple, continuous task such as the hands being not too tense, we accomplish a shift of the available attention away from the busy, noisy, talkative mind. This is because where we place the attention determines where we expend our energy. Much of our daily life is spent spinning in the head, thinking, thinking, thinking about all sorts of things from the past or the future. Shifting the awareness to the sensation of the hands and the whole moment becomes an experience with a different taste. Internally, we move closer to the moment. We change. Discovering the sensation of the hands on the shopping cart, the attention shifts to a more physical and stabilizing mode of being. When the attention can be directed to a useful, beneficial source it is less likely to be involved in distracted mind-wandering. In disciplines from prayer, meditation, martial arts, or visualization, the body is always a starting point for making us available to the spirit. It is a common thread that weaves through all spiritual disciplines.

Fourth, this act of attending to the tension in the hands is an intentional choice that in and of itself exercises the attention and strengthens its function. We have previously discussed the "muscle" of the attention and the need it has of being toned and disciplined. With its roots in the Latin word for pupil, *discipline* is a word that suggests openness to learning—its meanings need not be limited to harsh, threatening, or militaristic connotations. Discipline creates a certain order that allows things to work well. It is an act of deep compassion to our spiritual well-being to value the possibilities that come with discipline of the attention. We become more available to the sacred element if we understand that we are in need of practices which strengthen, organize, and open the pathways that can reveal to us the deeper side of life. By intentionally seizing the opportunities of the diverse ordinary circumstances that living affords us, like pushing a cart in a supermarket, we can take optimum advantage of our time here to open to spirit. Our deeper yearnings are able to be turned to viable spiritual practice all day long.

Fifth, the simplicity of being aware of hand tension when pushing the cart gives us something accessible and retrievable. A supermarket, like a microcosm of life in general, can be demanding and full of distractions. It is more than likely that we will be distracted and forget about our original intention with the hands. However, it is relatively easy to return to our original decision to practice this little task should we realize that we have forgotten. We believe that the attention is capable of continuity, when in fact continuity is elusive. It needs practice. The continuity we seek is similar to the continuity of spirit, the oneness that never ends. Continuity is reflected in life through the senses, the heartbeat, and the generations of people that inhabit the earth. We can connect to that continuity by starting with ourselves. When we lose the sense of continuity, it is not difficult to reaffirm a small thing like the sensation of the hands. We all doze off, but our strength lies in our ability to reawaken and strengthen our resolve.

Viewing the supermarket as a place to "work out," a gymnasium for the spirit, we wake up and develop our spiritual muscles. The cycle of remembering and forgetting and remembering again reflects a beneficial effort taking place by practicing awareness to our advantage and in service to a higher good. We have to go shopping, in any case. Why not use the time to awaken the consciousness and strengthen the spiritual musculature?

Learning from Limitations

Not needing to win any prizes or gain great inner peace in such an exercise, it is the serious effort that is important. Resolving to do active shopping, we may later realize that we have entirely forgotten the exercise, having gone to sleep somewhere between the dairy department and the condiments section. Have you ever experienced driving along a highway and "coming back" to find that the last many miles of driving you were totally somewhere else in your mind? Driving on automatic pilot, it was your automatic self, not your alert self who was driving the car. You were not "with it." Spinning in your head, you were leaving the driving to just happen, come what may. But the witnessing of our inattention is a positive and highly useful event, disturbing though it might be. It is a message, showing us that the muscle of attention needs to be exercised and reestablished. In fact, strange but true, the very act of noticing this lack of constancy in ourselves actually engages and strengthens the very same attention we wish to access. For most of us, access to the moment is more easily said than done, requiring strength, commitment, and the growth of skills that are only available through effort. Otherwise, we can spend a lifetime wondering, reading, seeking, never having done the inner tasks needed for some real change, some openness to the larger picture.

As in the development of any skill, we meet our limitations on the way. In learning a new skill, we meet ourselves face to face, and we are not always pleased with what we discover. But growth toward spiritual well-being occurs on a level quite distinct from the place where ordinary preferences occur. Spiritual discernment and preference has a different quality, a different taste. More impartial and nonjudgmental than our likes and dislikes, it doesn't exaggerate or explain or complain. It is a witness to our experience. This is not to say that we do not have or acknowledge our negative states or our manias and bravados. We do and we must, for what we are is precisely what we have been given to work with. Neither judging nor congratulating ourselves for our states, we simply notice. Again, we impartially witness.

Remember, our lack of skills in this area should not hurt our sense of worth. We are all struggling with who we are, whether we're conscious of it or not. Looking upon such struggles with compassion, our search is not one of despair, but of hope and possibility.

Grateful in the Grocery

While it takes a little time, effort, and understanding to become confident in the spiritual strength we have been given to develop, we know that, eventually, we can improvise. Suggestions here are offered as guidelines, not dogmas.

You might choose to do active shopping with an interest in the *feeling* dimension of the spirit. Remember, the attention can be mobilized in many ways toward spirit. What is most important is that we be intentional, that the attention be directed consciously. A good thought or feeling can be quite purposeful and directed.

For example, taking some broccoli off the vegetable shelves and placing it in your shopping cart can be a moment of intention and feeling. What would happen if, as you took the broccoli in your hands, you thought of the gift of food, passed down through many processes into your hands. Consider the miraculous process of creation: It takes rain, clouds, farmers, seeds, workers, truckers, sun, insects, soil—an endless list—to make a bunch of broccoli. A moment of appreciation with such a thought can bring sanctity, beauty, the sacred oneness right into our lives. Perhaps we will even be led, then, through this thought to a moment of gratitude, a penetrating and all-too-rare experience in most people's lives. So much of what we have and sustains us is taken for granted unless it is taken away from us. This is the direction of prayer and worship, where the attention is turned toward deeper appreciation leading to gratitude.

Each of us has different areas of interest that come with who we are. They are reflections of the individuality that has been given to us to work within and throughout our journey. Some of us are more intellectual, others more feeling, and others more physical. Yet we all have some of these things in our makeup. Sometimes it is easiest to go with what is most suited to our nature, and sometimes it feels right to turn to a side of ourselves that is not often exercised. This is not always clear, but we can usually tell if we are on the right track by an honest look at the quality it brings to our life. We need to try things on for size and see if they fit.

There will be many more approaches to accessing the moment and the spiritual dimension in life presented in the rest of this book. Any suggestions are by no means written in stone. They are examples to show how this accessing works, so that our personal predilections and styles can create means of helping ourselves to be more present, more conscious of living in the moment.

A Sacred Honor

Certain elements are essential to most spiritual traditions, contained in personal and communal ritual practices. Most paths to spirit enjoin us to go against our ordinary habit and do or be something out of the ordinary. We are asked to stay alert, be aware, move consciously, feel differently, speak more consciously, be still or be attentive to one thing or another. So too can we ask ourselves to try something different, to turn the attention to something else besides what is average and typical of our ordinary life. We might ask ourselves to shift the sensation, the mentality, the breath, or the feeling perspective. Whether it be prayer, meditation, visualization, service or study—whatever the route—effort is required for whatever discipline we take on in the name of spirit. This is true for the vast majority of spiritual and religious practices. So, too, do they ask us to focus and control our attention on whatever means or approach they offer. This inner effort we make is perhaps the most important part of the sacred journey and the attention is a common denominator regardless of the path.

If the spiritual dimension to our existence feels inaccessible, logic tells us that there is something about our own state of affairs that is preventing openness. It would be absurd to speak about creating sacredness, since the oneness is already there. Yet we do have a role in making our vessels, our hearts, our minds, and our bodies receptive to what we intuit, beckoning to be present in our lives.

The coming chapters in this book will present a wide range of options for the spiritual seeker. Thoughts, feelings, the body, and our dream life will be explored as they relate to the world of spirit.

As previously mentioned, part of the error of modernity is the disproportionate amount of material readily available to the seeker. Information is only useful if applied. When we read something that strikes an important chord, we often let it drift away like another captivating movie or a moving passage of music. Failing to act upon what is inspirational, useful or important is a sad loss. If it touches you, follow through. Sacred attention, our gift from the divine, is a privilege that is honored by concrete inner activity and honest efforts. In the world of spiritual possibility, efforts speak louder than words.

Chapter 3

———— ✥ ————

THE HEART OF
THE MATTER

Do we receive from the world for ourselves? Yes. Only for our-selves? No. Receiving sunlight and water, a field of thirsty potato plants thrives, a farmer makes his living, and a nation of people is fed. Hearing a symphony, a child is enthralled, a life interest in music is sparked, a genius is nurtured. Four decades later, now an adult, this same child conducts his own orchestra, three more children in the audience are deeply enthralled, three more lives become dedicated to music, millions get to hear beauty, and the ceaseless cycle of artistry spirals through time.

Traveling through life in our own unique style, we are all designed to interact and contribute to the sacred network within which we exist. From the point of view of spirit, we are not so much receivers as we are, like Creation, pure givers. It is our task as individuals to sustain and further life with as much commitment as we can muster. By listening to this call, we reconnect to spirit in life. Our essence is service through giving and our method is kindness and compassion.

Stoking the fires of our own life are food, oxygen, shelter, the warmth of human companionship, and the care others have for us. But this fuel is not given to us to be hoarded or withheld, but rather for service to something greater than ourselves. All energy, whether plant, animal, or human consciousness, is given to pass along, through the service of our existence, using what we need to sustain ourselves for this task. In this way we contribute positively and consciously to the cycle of eternity. Requiring our own happiness and physical well-being so that we can be a sharing participant in the immediacy of the world, we are continuously encouraged by our deepest and often most submerged impulses to give freely and intelligently of our capacities, no matter how grand or humble.

You're stuck on the side of the interstate with a flat tire. The drive to a state park for a small picnic is put on hold until the tire is changed. There are four passengers in the car: you, your aunt, and your two younger cousins. There's no help as far as the eye can see. You are the only one who knows how to change a flat tire, so you roll up your sleeves. The nuts on the wheel, holding the tire in place, are too tight. They won't budge. Tired and hungry when you started, the indifferent heat of the summer afternoon oppressive, your wise aunt urges you to stop, come over to the shade of the tree. There, on a blanket you join everyone else for a break, you eat fruit and have a cold drink. Jokes and mirthful barbs are exchanged about the bumpy course of the journey. No one has lost heart, trusting that eventually the prearranged rendezvous in the park with the other relatives will happen, just a little later than expected. Food had been brought along for the picnic, and there is plenty. Eating, sitting under a tree with your aunt and cousins, and drinking iced tea is renewing. Strengthened and revived, returning to the car, changing the flat tire awaits completion. You manage to get the bolts off the wheel, this time calmer, using intelligence and leverage with the wrench rather than mere brute strength. Within twenty minutes you are back on the road, the flat tire changed, the task completed. The journey continues, no one waiting at the family reunion in the state park even suspecting you had been delayed.

The food and drink gave pleasure and needed fuel. The warmth of relatives nourished inner resources to get the job done. But in the final analysis, the ultimate destination of all this nourishment was not your own enjoyment and pleasure. It was beyond your own need, your own desire, for it concerned the other people in the car you were driving and the relatives waiting for your arrival in the state park. You were looking to give appropriately to the situation and for this you needed strength. Nourishment and joy were given to you precisely because you were called to serve a situation involving other people's well-being, not merely your own. To serve a larger goal, whether we identify that goal as another person or the divine, is our spiritual need. It promotes life in the world and brings genuine satisfaction to our existence. All journeys through life follow this sacred order. It is this principal that embodies the spiritual impulse of service, kindness, compassion, and caring. We receive for the ultimate purpose of imparting and sharing, contributing what comes through us to a magnanimous divine scheme.

Giving to our world is the supreme spiritual model. Like the sun sending out the essential light sustaining organic life, there exists an unlimited source of divine intention sustaining creation. The cycles of birth and death, growth and decay, joy and tribulation are the way of Creation. Eternally shaping and reshaping what exists, the divine intention carries no craving, no malice, yet it poses a serious challenge for us, for we are beings sharing time and space with others on a small and fragile planet.

The problems plaguing human existence, the distortions of a pure life-giving impulse, are the results of our choices. Human suffering is, for the most part, a reflection of the human will gone awry. For the divine intention has fashioned us to choose life over disintegration and wisdom over stupidity. Creation is putting out a sustaining effort, a pure giving, perhaps even rooting for us, in the hope that we will choose the least disruptive road to the realization of who we truly are and what our sacred mission is.

Spiritually constructed according to the same laws governing Creation, our actions are part of a continuity that never yields its integrity or autonomy. We can fight it or enjoin it, but either way, this divine continuity triumphs. It is our choice as the human race whether we suffer discord or harmonize with the cosmic scheme. Our awareness and decisions use our senses, feeling, sensation, body, and mind for either selflessness or selfishness. We are continuously serving one or the other. As life is under the umbrella of Creation, our organism's sacred journey is under the umbrella of our attention and finally, the choices we make to give or not to give.

Kindness, giving, or compassion are the keystones holding up the arch of the spiritual realm. They contain within them all the elements necessary for bringing the sacred into our world, for accessing divinity within the daily challenge. Neither kindness nor giving occur without our effort and alertness. A study with nuance and layers, the practice of kindness and giving has many faces, encouraging self-examination and attentiveness to ourselves and the world.

Self-Transcendence

An act of giving has the unusual capacity of transcending our personal preferences. One of the purest transformational gifts we have received, kindness and other forms of giving allow us to leap beyond our limited subjectivity into a more global sense of the oneness pervading everything. It becomes us to be kind and giving, providing an opportunity to see and feel another's moment as we feel our own. This empathy brings a new dimension into focus, one in which the universality of being human truly resides.

As spiritual beings we have within us something like a tuning fork. If we strike one tuning fork that is the same as another, both vibrate at the same frequency. In the same fashion we resonate with other people's joys and sorrows. Empathizing with another person's humanness, we feel the interconnectedness that, until this sharing, we may have only cursorily accepted as truth. Responding to need, we place our own resources at the behest of Creation, allowing the purpose of our life at that moment to be defined in its most sacred terms. Always seeking a way to impart and serve, the giving intention is the spirit's most penetrating way to survive its journey on Earth. Never intended to be neglected or left out of the cyclical equation, nourishing the world we also feed ourselves, thus demonstrating the respect Creation has for the faculties we have been temporarily given "on loan." Overseeing ourselves, we are alive for the greatest well-being of all existence.

The Opportunities of Sacrifice

Sacrifice has always been at the heart of spiritual discipline. Unfortunately, contemporary culture has misconstrued sacrifice to mean simply a form of deprivation or denial of one's own needs. The fear of sacrificing our own convenience is the major obstacle to kindness and giving. Sacrifice in the direction of spirit is the letting go of a personal desire to be available for a more significant need. It never denigrates and always elevates the self. In its original spiritual meaning, sacrifice is a ceremony or order of sacredness. An act connecting us to the divine, it comes in peace.

A close friend of many years, running into serious difficulty in her life, seeks out your attention and care. You devote hours practically helping and supporting her in her particularly hard struggle. It is not always a pleasant task, seeing the rough edges of life and being with her in a time of compelling need. Also, her need for companionship cuts into some other things you would do and people you would see. Basically, however, you truly have no complaints. Usually capable of sacrificing certain aspects and desires of your existence to be there for someone else, you also attend to your needs, but temporarily let go of some convenience and ease in your own life. Making sure that you don't neglect your own existence, there is plenty of room to give up some "wanting" and sacrifice some pleasure for service. In the end, all Creation benefits from this choice of yours. Such purposeful sacrifice of comfort requires no sentimentality, needs no plaintive violins or extra drama, but only a willingness to respond genuinely from the place in the heart that makes space for another.

Within our own private existence, we show kindness toward ourselves and those dependent on us by making choices that sacrifice destructive habits for constructive ones in our daily life. These are choices of the spirit, challenging us in different ways each day. For example, we have made a decision to avoid a certain food, convinced that it is not in the best interests of our well-being. The craving remains, but through an act of kindness and giving to ourselves, we choose sacrifice, leaving that portion of our desire behind as we aim for the greater goal, the soundness of body. Here a spiritual principle is at work, encouraging us toward a generosity of spirit that never feels deprivation. Fear of not having, of not maintaining our coffers, desperately holding on to the small pleasures that come our way, disappear in the presence of an abiding compassion and giving that includes ourselves as well. Giving and compassion, no matter the source or goal, eventually proves itself to be the source of a much more reliable bounty of happiness. By focusing this way on the letting go of anything we need to give up or sacrifice for whatever reason, we immediately connect to a spiritual support system that dispels fear. For what appears in purposeful sacrifice to be a loss is a gain of spiritual importance.

The Kindness of Strangers

A caring attitude does not come easily to some of us. Stressed out by modern life, many of us move into our fears and avoid certain encounters, when kindness and giving can define the tenor of a moment.

You are approached by a homeless street person asking for money. Those of us living in big cities have had to grapple with the decision of when it is appropriate to give or not. A very few just give because they were asked. Others give, for to not give would be too uncomfortable. They don't want to do the wrong thing, and feel guilty, and so they give. There are those who are annoyed and angry at the homeless, who feel that they shouldn't have to be confronted with another's destitution on a daily basis. Some of us don't want to give, fearing we are supporting an addict, and so stigmatize even the just plain hungry. We know of some who do volunteer work with the homeless who made a decision not to give to panhandlers, believing sincerely that giving to a panhandler supports a wrong societal approach to helping people. In any event, everyone has an opinion and a point of view. Regardless of the moment, we can act kindly by acknowledging that another exists and is a human being just the same as ourselves. We can give with kindness and we can refuse with kindness. It is beneath us as humans to treat a request as if it wasn't made.

There certainly exist times when intentionally ignoring someone is the only option we feel we have. On occasion someone perceives another person as dangerous, perhaps due to drugs or mental instability. But it is the exception, not the rule. We can treat a person with gentleness and kindness, rather than act in a dismissing way. Not as a tragedy but as a person. Choosing not to give, we can also show some compassion by saying something like: "I am not giving any money." Even when we say no to someone's request, we can say yes to their existence. Acknowledging another's humanness can occur with a well-meaning glance, an honest hello, or a simple gesture, even when we don't give them what they want or help in a material way. Help can come in many forms and the least we can do is not be hurtful.

It takes a certain amount of initiative for some us to show kindness to a person who is checking out the groceries, driving the bus, or waiting on our table in a restaurant. Most of us are too self-absorbed to acknowledge another's service with due respect and care. These days there is a lack of education and training in social skills that were once customary, and service workers are not always friendly. But we can be kind, even if they may not be or seem shut down to minimal contact. Life can be hard, and if we haven't walked in another's shoes, we can't judge. Here we have the spiritual potential of making connections to the web of life by appreciating another's humanity and being interested more in enlightening the situation than just reacting to it. A simple "Hi" or "How are you" or whatever comment or gesture of kindness and care arises spontaneously can be as helpful to the world as rain to parched soil.

Is that passing consideration of another's humanness a spiritual matter? It certainly is. Even amenities such as holding the door for another person are the mechanical norms established as behavior which respects the spirit. The social order has a lot of problems and errors in it, but it is not always wrong. By showing even the most average courtesy, and doing it with awareness and a sense of responsiveness to the world, we are connecting to spirit in life.

Another's Shoes

Responsible empathy is the ability to feel another's situation, to imagine ourselves being in their shoes. A deeply and surely sensed phenomenon of the spirit, empathy allows human feeling to translate into a compassionate condition of the heart. As a feeling, empathy can become stuck by turning into an emotion. As mentioned in chapter 1, feelings are present tense. They concern what is happening, not what has been, and they have no story line connected to them. Emotions are responses that are triggered by an external stimulus and then take on a life of their own, playing old messages and themes stored in us from our past experiences and feelings. Emotions tend to cloud our life path, but feelings tend to move and guide us forward in the most useful direction. Confronted with another's pain, our feeling for their suffering is the wellspring of connection to the moment. We are called upon to leave our own emotionality out of the situation, in favor of feeling and sensation. Otherwise, our own agenda, our own fears and preferences can seriously erode our capacity to be with another's circumstance. Feeling and intelligence working together allow us to be of service. We are then in a condition of "response-ability" and can make choices from a place of true respect for the current circumstance. It is a worthwhile study to learn to distinguish between what the heart tells us immediately, and the stories we create from our own past that create emotions. Our life is in the here and now, continuously informed by what we feel.

There is a joke: "A Boy Scout took an elderly gentleman on a walker across the street. The only problem was, the elder didn't want to cross." This is kindness gone awry. The Boy Scout's impulse to help had lost its spontaneous ethos and had become mechanical, rendering it absurd rather than beneficial. The helping impulse needs a certain monitoring in us so that it can hit its mark and serve. Our whole intelligence is necessary and our attention and alertness to the present is required.

Someone is crying, sobbing deeply. You move toward her and put your arm around her shoulder. At that moment, you feel her stiffen. She inhales and seems to hold on to her breath. Where before, she seemed relaxed in the crying state, her body is now tense, on alert. You have interrupted her mourning, her way of comforting herself, her release of pain. Yet, you acted out of kindness; it was a natural, well-meaning gesture, to move toward someone and offer comfort in this way.

An arm around the shoulder is comforting for some people, but not for everyone. The giving and acceptance of various forms of kindness is a personal, private matter. How do we know which form of "kindness" to offer? By being sensitive to the cues sent out to us. Staying open and sensitized to the feedback is important, for it gives the right shape and content to what we say or don't say, do or don't do. We need to move from the heart but with a witness and awareness that can appreciate and respond to the situation with maturity of vision. There is a whole environment of conditions operating in any moment that needs to be seen and taken into account when we act. We can ask ourselves the question: What "help" will help?

A young, enthusiastic and caring social worker told us how she learned a very important lesson about helping people. It was her first job and she loved older people. She was in a nursing home. Seeing someone sitting alone in her room disturbed her. She was thinking of loneliness and abandonment—"She has suffered this too long and I will help." Entering the older woman's private room, the social worker implored, "Go into the day room with the others, join the activities, talk to other people." She cajoled, encouraged, and even insisted. The resident stayed firm. Finally, the young woman came to her senses. It dawned on her that this older woman actually liked being alone; it had always been her way, and she was not about to change. She realized how she had come into the situation with her own view of what it meant to be kind. Newly aware, she honored the older woman's way of being in the world and gathered a new understanding of giving.

To know what is considered kind to someone else, there is a simple formula: Ask! There is a children's game called "May I?" that involves taking steps, but before you do so, you ask, "May I?" If you neglect to ask permission, you are tagged as "out." That what one loves, another dislikes is a fact worth carrying with us along with our care. This principle of giving is clearly demonstrated in gift giving. Selecting a present for someone's birthday, if it is done consciously, is not about buying what we like, but rather taking into account his likes and tastes, even if his preferences are at odds with your own. It is a sign of consideration and respect for the diversity of humankind to approach all giving with a magnanimity of caring that transforms our need to give into meaningful generosity.

Ultimate Giving

In recent years it has become an axiom of social programs designed for the economically disenfranchised to provide the means for people to earn a living by their own labor and efforts. Encouraging people to be endlessly dependent on meager governmental charity has proven to be fraught with limitations. Effective help does often require more effort and sophistication than we are inclined to readily give.

In the workplace we meet similar needs. A new employee has joined the staff, and he is adjusting to the new work environment just as you did when you were first hired. Empathetic to his efforts to be part of the flow of work and responsibility in the office, you are friendly and kind, aiming to be helpful. But you can choose from two kinds: help and better help. You can fix the problem on his computer with the click of a few buttons familiar to you but unknown to him. That's helping. But you can also take two extra minutes to explain how to fix it himself next time, giving the patience, care and extra time necessary to make him free of an unnecessary dependency. That is better helping. It is also a sound and practical way for an office to function, but that doesn't mean it's not a spiritually significant act. It simply means that what is good for your own spirit and the spirit of another is good for all. Extending yourself to another and stretching your giving to include the question, "What is the best help?" is the surest way to ultimate giving. There, right in the middle of the moment, in ordinary life, you intersect with the divine will, asking you to help the flow of the river of existence to pass freely along its preferred, unobstructed path.

The Practice of Anonymous Giving

There is nothing wrong with enjoying the act of giving. However, in spiritual terms, we run up against the personal problem of distinguishing our own self-satisfaction and egoism from purer motives. The world needs all forms of charity, so it would be ill-advised to simply not give to someone or an organization because it is too pleasurable for us to do so or because making a financial donation gives us a swelled head. Either way, the money is needed. It is to our spiritual advantage, then, to ponder our own motives for giving. By seeking to grow and learn from this, we can constantly purify the skills needed for truly compassionate giving. It is simply a question of self-reflection and examination done with honest spirit and an inquiring mind. We each need to find our own way to meet this challenge, should its importance strike us as spiritually useful.

There is probably no act we do that is entirely free of selfish motivations, but there arises now and then a way to sidestep our ego's craving for credit and praise. This is by giving charity or help anonymously, in such a way that no one else knows the source of a gift of needed money, for example. It becomes a bit complicated to do this fully in our culture due to checks being identifiable and the seduction of the tax structure that encourages us to make receipts and take financial advantage of our charitable gifts. But occasions can arise, and where there is a will there is a way. There is nothing to stop us from slipping money under someone's door with a note thanking them for the opportunity to help. Again, the logistics can be problematic, and it is often simply not possible, but appropriate situations do arise. Sometimes a variation on the theme can be done through a third party, although someone else's knowledge makes the gift not strictly anonymous. Arising at times is the circumstance of someone desperately in need whose pride may make it painful for them to receive.

Anonymity of the giver may just be a bit helpful, if not the perfect solution.

The Compassion of the Broken Heart

Eighteenth-century Rabbi Nachman of Breslau (now in Poland) told his students that it is forbidden to be depressed but required to be heartbroken. Heartbreak happens to most people. Whether it is the sudden death of a loved one or a shattered relationship which is the apparent trigger, heartbreak is a feeling that is given to us to create a more compassionate world.

When one's heart is broken, the overwhelming pain has a singular poignancy. Experiencing vulnerability and openness, there is a raw quality to the feeling that cracks open the heart and breaks down one's separation from the world. Unfortunately, we often allow ourselves to move from the brokenhearted feeling into the destructive emotion of depression. Depression is the opposite of a broken heart. It is a shutting down of our ability to love, give, and share in an interconnected world. The energy gets stuck inside and we withdraw from life. On the other hand, heartbreak, often the prevalent feeling surrounding a loss, actually puts us in a subtle state of deep surrender to the divine, unbearable though the circumstances may be. The people one meets one can suddenly feel in a different way, sensing the universality of the human condition and the truth of our collective vulnerability. It is one of the rare experiences in life when the veil that usually separates one's heart from the rest of the world drops away. Standing naked, pure and intensely real in our feelings within the present moment, the universe helps us absorb more deeply the nature of compassion and the fabric of oneness that is everything. If we are fortunate, and we don't allow the closing off of the self into depression, we are initiated into a new, enriching connection with others—a connection informed with an empathy and care that is like no other we've experienced before. We also learn a new kindness toward ourselves, being, as we are, also part of the ineffable web.

Chapter 4

MINDING OUR MIND

How much thought does it take to smell a flower? How much thinking is required to see a tree?

Lying on white sand and listening to the ocean, you're happy that you finally got away from it all. Yet, despite the freedom, the calming sounds, the plaintive squawk of a distant gull, the penetrating warmth of the sun and the vastness of the beach, your mind continues to chatter and converse with itself. Discussing likes and dislikes, projects, reveries, personalities and incidents from the past, you finally doze off.

This is the way we are much of the time. At work, at home and even in play, thinking—that tremendously useful tool—has become our prime energy expenditure, consuming our attention at every turn. Simply put, we deplete ourselves by thinking at the wrong times, when thought is not necessary. Then, when clear thinking is needed, we lack the focus and reserve for the best we can give. Our brain becomes overtaxed, overstimulated and overwrought, wreaking havoc on the body and the emotions as well.

Attempting to find some respite, we try every kind of human invention to dull the experience of relentless thinking. Unfortunately, some of us go into addictions, only to find they are a spirit-enslaving dead end. Encountering a good vacation, a fine movie, the birth of a child, a special moment with a friend or loved one catapults us into a positive state of mostly happy and upbeat thoughts. But happy states induced by outside events simply don't last. Sooner or later we are confronted once again with our own thoughts running us ragged.

Unseen and always informing life, a more sacred presence appears to be in hiding. It is not hiding. Rather, it is merely obscured by a curtain of unnecessary and ever chattering thoughts. The wandering mind, weaving speculations, fantasies, worries, diversions, obsessions, expectations, and noise—all this is pretty stiff competition for a more spiritual focus.

Like a symphony concert in the park drowned out by jet planes flying overhead, our capacity to listen to and appreciate life on its simplest and most profound terms is overwhelmed by the ceaseless presence of thought. It is a significant part of our spiritual challenge to find an approach that frees us from this condition and clears our way of needless mental debris.

Putting Thought in Its Place

Thought is a tool that helps us figure things out. We use it to negotiate our way in the world, to reason, deduce, infer, associate one thing with another, and shape our existence. With reason we invent, build homes, schedule appointments, and organize most of ordinary life. Thought is a tool that drives technology and creates solutions to problems. It calculates, figures, memorizes, builds civilizations—and sometimes destroys them. (Most if not all of the violence and ecological devastation in the world is the tragic end result of thought run amok.) We need to be very clear on this point: Thought, with all of its strengths, is not an enemy; for thinking comes in peace, created to coexist with the larger sense of who we are. It is not in our personal or collective interest to diminish the importance of thought. This can lead to serious error. Our task, from the point of view of spiritual practice, is *to put thought in its proper perspective* so that it remains a servant and not a master.

Imagine owning a useful tool—a measuring tape, for example—and holding on to it all day long, measuring your shoes before you put them on, measuring your baked potato before you eat it, measuring your toothbrush in order to brush your teeth. Sounds absurd? This is what we do with our thinking. Or perhaps we can say this is what our thinking does *to* us. It reverses its place in our life and drowns out the simplicity and truth in much of our experience. Thought has become something more than what it was given to be. Like measuring the baked potato on our plate, it is misplaced, complicating what is essential and overstepping its otherwise useful purpose.

Used productively, the same measuring tape can show one's waist size when being fitted for a suit, or measure the length of a couch to see if it will fit in a new apartment. Just as this clever tool, useful and in service to life, can hinder if not in proper perspective, so too does thought eminently serve humanity when applied appropriately.

Have you ever stood in front of an unusually beautiful painting in a museum? Something strikes you about the entire canvas, this whole field of form and color a harmonious whole. For a moment, just a fleeting moment, you are struck. Stillness pervades within a sacred pause; who you are is reduced to sensation and feeling, beyond thought, personality and name. Unconditioned experience of color, shape, balance, and detail happens without obstructive thinking. Without struggle, without attempting to stop thought, to kill it, or control it, a large gap in the web of thinking has appeared instantaneously, allowing us to taste who we are, and who we are not. The "me" has become more universal and less self-centered. No longer just a lone blade of grass, we are now part of a spiritual ecology, part of that meadow where the vastness of creation unfolds. Spontaneously, thought has moved aside. A deeper clarity has penetrated the din of thinking.

Within daily life as well, following the light beam of awareness leads to a quieting or lessening of the power of thought. Neither a quick-fix technique nor a mental game, an internal process is readily available to us to work with and build upon. Fueling life to keep the gates of spirit open and available to us requires a patience with ourselves and a deep wish to live in a moment differently. Most importantly, it requires an effort of our attention and an honest willingness to shift gears into a fuller appreciation of the depth of existence.

Noticing the Space Before Thought

Useful thinking makes a formidable contribution to our ability to function in and contribute to our world. Learning how much water, flour, sugar, and salt is necessary to bake a loaf of bread, how to knead it, let it rise, how to shape it and place it in the oven at the correct temperature, we know something new.

Unnecessary thinking—thinking that obscures our experience and complicates a simple moment—is different. It is not productive. Rather than adding something to our life, it detracts from it. The skill we can develop to counter unnecessary thinking requires alertness. It's about noticing the movement of thought.

Let's suppose you live in a congested urban environment. You are reading in your living room. All of a sudden, a car alarm goes off in the street outside. For an instant you wonder what is this piercing sound, then you recognize it's a car alarm. As quickly as a few blinks of the eye, an internal dialogue begins. *I hate those car alarms! If only they would ban them. This is the third time tonight. I hate living in the city. I want to move to the country. I never should have listened to my cousin and gotten this job here in the first place . . .* and on and on.

Let us return to the beginning of our scenario. The penetrating sound from the car alarm has entered our ears. There is a conditioned response, composed of thoughts, preferences, and opinions stored inside our memory bank, in the program of our computer. Between the time when the sound first hits us, impacting on our nervous system, and when the programmed internal dialogue of thoughts begin to chatter, there is a space, a gap between the event and our *thinking about* the event. Like the stillness before a storm, it is a space that we can dwell in. We can see it, live it, feel it, taste it. It is a moment in which it's *possible* to connect to the timeless. For in that instant, becoming alertness itself, we are garnering the strength and vitality that come from the mysterious portion of our existence. An ordinary moment becomes a seminal moment, while our name, birth date, who we are becomes insignificant. The habitual way of being caught in the thinking hasn't yet occurred. In this moment we can be present to the fullness of being. Within this space preceding thought, there is an alertness and an experience that is happening, energy rich and full of the essence of the world.

Can we notice this space? Can we live in this space, before mental comments have set in? Were we alert when the thinking started? Did we notice it? Were we *present* for it?

These are questions we need not answer either affirmatively or even with words; for they are part of a practice, a study, a silent inquiry into our nature as human beings. What counts more than any expected result is making the appropriate effort. Expecting a result, we bring the same interfering thoughts into play which we aim to get beyond. Don't try to accomplish or gain anything with this type of process, simply "dial direct." Simply notice with alertness and calm interest and reside there for a short yet timeless moment, in the gap before the thinking comes in.

A good place to practice this is the first moment when you wake up in the morning. See if you can find an inner watchfulness that can be present when you first return to the waking state from the world of sleep and dreaming. There is a very pure moment there, like a dawning of consciousness, when the impressions of the morning light and the room are actually very available with a minimum of thought. Many of us will only find this available on a day off from work, when we don't use an alarm clock, so that the waking moment is more natural and rhythmic. But even during the days when the alarm clock rings, you can *mind your mind,* to see if you can notice that space, that gap before thought. Can you move from this inner awareness and shut off the alarm clock without completely losing yourself to the inevitable flood of thoughts and opinions that flood us in response? Even your annoyance or frustration at having been awakened does not occur immediately. It might appear that way at first, but you need to find out, for there is also a gap, a space before thought enters and begins its monologue.

Practicing this regularly has profound implications for understanding one's mind and the spiritual side of life. Again, it is the quality and the constancy of the effort that bears fruit. Keeping at it is the most important part. We can't blame it on a busy schedule, for it takes no time out of our life. We are simply shining the light beam of our awareness to observe the movement of thought.

Alertness is a form of renewal. It helps us to live present tense. The newness inside is really renewal, making the present fresh, letting the past be the past and moving on into the portable now.

Any moment can be the moment when we intentionally renew our relationship to the world. Particularly fertile is the time when something new happens. Each day we walk out the door, we leave our home, and go forth into the world. This seemingly ordinary moment is a moment of change. We venture forth into the world, leaving the shelter of home and crossing the threshold into the outdoors. This is a perfect moment to be attentive and experience how the sights, sounds, and smells hit us when we take them in, the explosive quality of the daylight, or the softness of an overcast day. Rather than naming the experience or bringing past memories to it, pause for a second to see the movement of life, feel it and simultaneously notice the movement of your own thought. Invite yourself to abide in the space before the thoughts take over and before you start categorizing the experience or complaining about the weather. You are simply "being," experiencing what is happening. At that point, we enter into a place of greater honesty and relationship to our world. Again, it is a process of doing less by being more attentive and simple, so that you can appreciate the moment more fully, without immediate regard for your preferences. This does not mean you shouldn't go get another sweater if you feel you are underdressed for the weather. But we are speaking about a simplicity of view and experience that occurs in us before thoughts, likes, and dislikes enter. We direct our attention to the wish to notice, not to the desire to have a city without smog, or another sweater. That is different—a thought-out conclusion based upon experience. See if we can be in the space before such thinking enters for just ten seconds of our time. For therein awaits the sacred.

Cynthia has a busy schedule at work. She has three important phone calls to make, one after another, each contingent on the other in order to draw up a proposal and present it at a meeting next week. Working behind a closed door, she is totally immersed in her work and under a deadline. Concluding her third phone call, she decides to go to the coffee maker for a cup of coffee. She rises from her chair and opens the door. This is a perfect time to begin anew, to return home to the space before thought comes rushing in. When she opens the door, she enters a different space, a different world. She knows that there is a chance to find a momentary space in her thoughts, if she is willing to take the opportunity and pause for a moment, to watch and stay alert. Before moving on to the next part of her busy morning, she tunes in to herself as she opens the door, and becomes more aware. Recalling her spirit and becoming alert to the change, she pauses and takes in the new sounds, the new images, the hallway, which is a different space from her room. Seizing the opportunity, she feels a touch saner, if not actually quieter. Cynthia feels the rushing of the mind, the nervousness, the onslaught of thinking. But, having taken a valuable moment to consciously notice this, with intention and interest, perhaps she is a bit calmer. The key benefit resides in the effort.

What Cynthia did for herself was to distinguish who she is from her streaming, screaming thoughts. True, she found no miracles in the moment. But through her efforts she is subtly but surely building the necessary point of view for spiritual growth. Cynthia is in a process of learning to expend energy on behalf of her spiritual life. As was mentioned in the chapter on the attention, there is something like a muscle that is being exercised every time we become intentionally alert to what is happening inside. Like a steady but small flame, these efforts build a fire of awareness and spiritual intention that becomes increasingly reliable.

Minding your mind is not an end in itself but rather a means toward closer contact with the rich world around you and how you reflect that world. Our thinking has built too many fortresses around the kernel of who we are. It is with this kernel that we are able to meet life on its own terms.

Doing What Is Necessary

You are driving down a road and you get a flat tire. "Just what I needed! Now I'll never get there on time." You become annoyed and frustrated. Nervousness, irritability, fear, anger—all the obstacles that come from thinking show up and define what life is at that moment. Yet, difficult as things might appear, there is a way to struggle with the power of thought. Working right in the world of action, where reality is always changing and bringing events into our life, we can practice "doing what is necessary." By focusing on what has to be done in steps, with energy and intention, the rhythm of our inner life becomes much more focused and steady. "But," you might object, "I do what is necessary. I floss, I pay my taxes, and I am responsible in my human affairs." Responsibility for daily affairs is not to be scoffed at, for sure; it is a regularity that needs to go hand in hand with spiritual discipline. But we are speaking here of dedication. We dedicate the challenge in front of us to our spiritual growth. If you want to, you can say that to yourself, just like that. But then the work really begins.

Let's say you are going to change the tire yourself. You let your focus be on what you need to do next. Not on getting the task over with, avoiding experiencing the work, but on opening the trunk, getting the tire out, the jack, and the tools you'll need. Using your full intelligence and insisting on alertness, let each step unfold, moment to moment, task to task, with an eye on optimum simplicity and efficiency. Keep everything simple. What will no doubt occur will be the inevitable arising of thoughts that have no purpose except to distract you from your purpose. Notice these thoughts as distinct phenomena that are passing by, like a small plane pulling an advertising banner that is there for a moment but then is gone. They are thoughts. Temporary, they need be appreciated as such. One can simply notice their movement and urge the attention back to what is necessary right now. Pick a step in the process, like lifting the spare out of the trunk. Entering completely into the purity of action, let yourself do what is necessary to lifting the tire. Anything else, consider extraneous.

The way we are constructed, in much of our activity, we already understand the basics of what is required to do the task. For spiritual purposes, we focus completely on how we do it, rather than only on getting it done. Like good cooking, we must think, but only at certain moments. The rest is the care we bring to the process, the attention, or the love. So bask in the actions and let them be your foremost interest. When you notice the thoughts coming in talking about what you are doing, then you have ceased to do only what is necessary. Something extra and irrelevant has entered. But don't make a big tale about it. Just return once again to focusing on what you are doing and how well it can be done, simply, with the least expenditure of thinking. Decide on a course of action, leave thinking, and act.

Potentially highly meditative and spiritually useful as a conscious means of practicing being in the moment, even prying a hubcap off a car wheel can be done with care, interest, and calm, although it requires some physical strength. By applying that care, by doing only what is necessary, the impatient violence of our actions falls away, and the thinking process slows down.

The workplace, too, affords opportunities to "do what is necessary." What would it be like to choose one thing that you do frequently and do it with the same sense of commitment to inner study? One could choose the use of the photocopy machine and follow the same internal strategy. Pick a task that has a little action in it, like a cleaning-out routine. Choose a task that is a little physical—perhaps putting new paper in the photocopier, or replacing the print cartridge in your desktop printer. (At home, cleaning up the kitchen after using it or just folding some laundry would be ideal activities.) Then maximize your care, your efficiency and your awareness in doing the activity step by attentive step, and allow the thinking to be a secondary distraction, purposely and repeatedly bringing your attention back to the chore or action at hand.

Going a Little Bit Slower

Arising as an impulse from within ourselves, slowing down within an activity can be a useful tool when used with care. While our automatic thoughts often race at a furious and persistent rate, the speed at which we do most things in life is adjustable, allowing us to switch gears and break the momentum of the habitual. Affording us the opportunity to shift to a more aware mode, slowing down the speed of doing an activity need not be extreme.

In fact, virtually any conscious choice to slow down can potentially create the conditions for a new encounter with the moment. It is an easily accessed means to help us awaken to the presence of another possibility within existence.

Have you ever noticed that passengers often wake up from sleeping in the back seat of a car when the speed of the traveling vehicle noticeably slows down? The phenomenon is similar in our own bodies and spirits. Shifting speed, we awaken a slumbering consciousness by changing our ordinary "traveling velocity." The impulse to decelerate, however, needs to come from choice, from inside of us, from a wish to be different. A slowing down in the outer pace of life, while perhaps less stressful on our bodies, is in no way inherently meaningful for spiritual practice in and of itself. Even slowing down, if done in a reactive way or as an automatic gesture, can be consumed by the force of habit and feed the habitual, less aware part of our nature by becoming a mechanical act devoid of larger purpose.

Ultimately, what provokes us into greater alertness and consciousness is the source of spiritual productivity, not the speed of an activity. Unfortunately, spinning endlessly in unproductive thinking can occur regardless of the speed of the music we are dancing to. Slowing down, however, might provide a gateway to awareness and heightened sensitivity, if that is what we are sincerely interested in.

The momentum of the fast-paced mind runs ahead of our activity and pulls us this way and that. You need to reload the photocopy machine at work? Slow down. Care and attention just might surprise you and spontaneously arise within the frantic throws of a hectic day at work to remind you of a deeper part of life, where things are less dispersed. Slowing down can lead to a calming experience, where life becomes less of a fragment and more of a whole.

Speeding Up

There are also times when our thought weighs us down, causing our disposition to sag, hiding our alertness in the moment. There is the option, then, of speeding up the activity as a way of honoring the moment. Sometimes, consciously moving quicker than we might like to, we mobilize the energy we truly have available to us and infuse ourselves with freshness and life. It wakes us up and allows us to leap beyond a languid sense of hanging on to the past. Of course, one needs to do this at the right time, intentionally, not as a habit of going quickly and rushing whenever possible. Aiming to dehabituate the moment, we need to be creative in feeling out a way to engage the attention, the intention and the activity in the spirit of alertness and presence.

Creating Positive Resistance

Resisting a habit helps us to experience ourselves more profoundly and helps us to be more present and less involved in the thoughts that plague us. Many religions use the concept of giving something up as a spiritual practice or simply as a reminder of the sacred. We can do this personally, individually for our own spiritual growth. The concept of sacrifice in spiritual practice is at least partially connected to creating positive resistance to what is automatic in life, which obscures a multidimensional sense of the moment.

Certainly, when we do something against our moral sense or our conscience, we harm ourselves and the world in the process. But when we do something against our grain, against an unassuming habit, we enter into the realm of challenge, one of the locations where spiritual practice takes place and possibility unfolds. This friction, between the familiar and the unfamiliar, strengthens the personal will and helps to forge a more mobile and available attention. Our wish for spiritual connection can then be more frequently and effectively manifested, toward what matters most to our deeper self.

The thoughts that swim through us take up a lot of energy. They usurp our attention and take it away from the arena of choice. When we concretely go against a habit, the energy previously shunted to the thinking mind is shifted to the more conscious part of the brain. This change is to our spiritual benefit.

It helps deflate the importance of our automatic self and puts the conscious self in the forefront of the moment.

Perhaps it is your habit to always hold your coffee cup in your right hand. One could take it as a modest but nonetheless serious act of spiritual practice to drink your coffee for one week using your left hand. Take it as an experiment. You might find it much more profound than it sounds, for you will be shifted quite directly into a world where by resisting a commonplace habit one feels and experiences more of what is going on inside. This seemingly small step can be an entrée into expanded consciousness, for it takes attention and presence to do this consistently. See if it changes the stream of thought. "Thinking" might slow down a bit or even, for a moment, seem to disappear. Within this small act exist important elements of meditation, concentration, contemplation, self-knowledge, presence and awareness waiting to be discovered. Study this exercise and see if you notice anything. If nothing more, the effort allows one to see more profoundly just how strongly the force of the familiar has a hold on us. Our habits limit us to a small portion of ourselves and our world. Consciously meeting them only enriches our awareness of ourselves and our accessibility to an invisible reality.

There is no dogma involved in these endeavors. Any small habit you choose can be your own personal anchor to spiritual practice. Perhaps you always hang your coat in the same place in the closet. Hang it somewhere else for a week. Or you consistently pass around the front of your car to get to the driver's seat. Go around the back for a week. If you always put the right sock on first, put on the left. Do the same with the shoe and with tying the shoe. You'll quietly learn a lot about yourself by taking on such changes. But keep this practice to yourself; it loses something if you tell others what you are up to. Make it a private study between your ordinary self and the wish to be more connected to a larger picture, a greater awareness. Therefore, choose something small, not dramatic, but inwardly declare your commitment to the exercise for a given week and attempt it with fullness of heart. By anchoring one's inner work to a tangible task, we remind ourselves of being conscious, of taking a different road in life and inside our own consciousness. Does it help you calm down inside? Does it quiet you a little bit? Does it remind you of a sacred wish within the momentum of a busy life?

There is no need to go looking for the right time to practice being in the moment, for, like a string of pearls, life is one element after another, one activity after another occurring in the "now," always the right place to begin.

Imagining

Can you spare thirty seconds to try a simple imagery exercise? It very well might put you into a different mode, a calmer presence and a less agitated state of mind. Just as images appear as dreams when we sleep, so too do we have access to pictures and sensations when we close our eyes and perceive the pictures that are there.

As night dreams influence our state of mind when we awaken in the morning, waking internal imagery can be used in a similar way to transform our state in the immediate present.

This exercise takes no more than thirty seconds of your time. Its purpose is to significantly reduce the power of unnecessary thinking:

Sit upright. In a relaxed way, let your eyes close and allow them to remain closed for the duration of this exercise. Breathe out gently three times and then let the inhalation occur naturally. Emphasize the conscious, full exhalation done in three steps. In other words, breathe out, breathe out, breathe out, and then breathe in. Picture, feel, and experience yourself standing in a field. Suddenly in the sky, coming from the left of the horizon, there is the clamoring and squawking of a huge, haphazardly arranged flock of birds flying above that have come from the left side of the picture. They block out much of the sky. Watch them form a beautiful V formation and fly off gracefully to the right until they disappear. The sky is now crisp and clear, with no birds anywhere to be seen or heard. Know that your passing thoughts have gone. Don't dwell there. Just open your eyes. The exercise is now over. Give it a try and see if it doesn't place you in a clearer, more present state.

Here is another imagery exercise you can use. Its purpose is to help with clarity and presence. Try it also, at a different time and see if it helps you with clarity and presence:

Eyes gently closed, do the exhalation and inhalation the same way as in the other visualization. This time, however, picture a lovely clear glass vase on a beautiful wooden table. Half-filled with some stagnant water, it is holding some flowers that are dead and have dropped their dry petals on the table. Remove the vase, clean the table and quickly polish it so that the wood shines. Go to the kitchen sink, throw away the flowers, empty the stagnant water, wash the vase inside and out until it is immaculate and clear as can be. Let it glisten. Fill the vase with cool spring water and place it back on the table. Receive fresh flowers, your favorite kind, and place them in the vase. Notice their purity and beauty. The exercise is over. Now open your eyes.

These exercises are helpful to many people. See if you find them useful if and when you feel called to do them. They take but a moment, yet they connect us to the timeless world of spirit within the sacred presence of the "now."

Listening on Purpose

Even before we were born, we could hear. Unborn children seem to react to external sounds, music, the mother's voice, sometimes shifting positions and kicking in response to a symphony concert while in the womb. Hearing is a very rooted sense, linked to our own earliest origins of experience. Since the spiritual journey involves reconnecting to the source of our existence, listening provides a wonderful link to a condition of awareness that precedes thinking.

When a dog hears something new, his ears perk up and his listening is a perfect picture of attentiveness. Our sojourn with spirit, ever so closely involved with the attention and how it moves in life, can engage intentional listening in order to shift awareness, increase alertness and bring us more fully into the present moment.

Walking into a room, your mind preoccupied with the phone conversation you just had (the past), and the things you have to do later on (the future), thought has taken over. Just for a few seconds, attempt to listen on purpose. Each moment has a unique quality of sounds. Listening to the sounds, let their distinct qualities enter as purely as possible. Avoid naming them, giving them a label, other then the acceptance that they are sounds, not unlike listening to a piece of music. People's voices, papers rustling, steam pipes banging, rain falling, a television blaring, cars passing, the wind, one's own breathing. Treat them as different instruments in an orchestra of creation. Leave judgments or preferences for any particular sound. Try it for just a short moment. Even ten seconds will do. See if you can make it a level playing field, where one sound is as interesting as the next.

Again, beginnings are particularly accessible moments. For example, when you just enter or leave a house or a room, let the newness of the moment resonate through the experience of purposeful listening. The attention is then consciously engaged, and alertness and presence are momentarily reestablished. Unproductive thinking temporarily recedes because of a shift of focus. This strengthens and engages the attention, always the bottom line in spiritual work.

The part of ourselves that is listening purposefully, neither naming nor developing opinions about what we are listening to, is the conscious self, the aspect that is aligned with spirit.

The Way of the Appointment Book

Jam-packed with a million things to do, our life rolls on. Contemporary life styles are a complicated affair. A simple external life is rarely accomplished, even by the resolute who move to the country to grow their own food. Chores, tasks, responsibilities, people to contact, stores to visit, clients to call, forms to fill out, e-mail to retrieve, options to choose from—all conspire to offset our own taste of a simpler reality, a less cumbersome existence.

Much of the pressure that people feel in the face of the busy modern life is due to the problem of thinking about the future schedule, the perceived demands of the next few things that have to be done. Worry, anxiety, and pressure about what hasn't yet happened interfere with a simpler present, an active quietude. While connected to each other by the flow of time, every single scenario, event, or action exists in actuality as an autonomous fact, with no past and no future. Herein lies an essential spiritual paradox: Everything exists out of the dimension of time, while our consciousness that is experiencing events creates the notion of time. Time is really a spiritual question, for we feel creation in the present time, yet it is of the timeless.

Luckily for us, some very smart person invented the appointment book. They come in all shapes and sizes. There is even one that slides into your wallet and takes up about as much space as a credit card. One of the most helpful things we can do for our cluttered brains is to let the appointment book worry about what has to be seen to. Let the next thing that has to be done merely show up on your calendar. Fussing internally about the past or the future wreaks havoc on the present. Let the next thing come when it comes. Too many pictures and expectations and dreads, all forms of unproductive thinking, come from "handling" life that hasn't yet arrived. What has to be done now, we need to do. If what has to be done now is planning for a future birthday party for someone we love, then that is the present moment. But if you have decided to pick up the kids at 4 o'clock, use your appointment book and if necessary, set an alarm (they make them for the wrist, too) to tell you when it is 3:45. Then go pick them up. Too much thinking occurs in our lives due to this habit of worrying about a train that has yet to pull into the station of the moment. Render unto time what is time's, and it will yield more space for awareness, more room for tasting the truth of any given moment.

Chapter 5

―――――――――――

DREAMS, COURIERS OF THE DIVINE

Every night the dream world sends us powerful communiqués. While we often say, "I had this dream last night . . . ," we could just as easily say the dream had us. For a dream is like a parcel sent from an invisible source, delivered to us as we sleep. Its messages are sent to remind, to emphasize, to point something out, to inform, to wake us up to a truth. Dreaming, we are in the world of the visionary, a heroic drama complete with themes, setting, props, actions and a supporting cast. We are then living in a corresponding world, or "parallel universe," as real and present as the little girl Dorothy from Kansas on the yellow brick road to Oz.

The moment of the dream is not confined to time or space. This moment is when we meet a reality quite distinct, yet analogous, to our waking world. As with any other moment, it is there for us to acknowledge and appreciate with the illuminating fire of the human attention.

To dream is to receive a gift from a divine source. When we receive a gift, we are not obliged to bring it to someone else in order to examine its contents. Allowing its intelligence to enter our life, we might choose to share it with another; but the gift has been given to us alone to receive, understand, and embrace. Some of us have developed the erroneous belief that what we do with a dream is really a matter for the experts to judge. We have disowned the dream realm and the messages being sent, pleading ignorance and bequeathing our own authority to specialists. But the dream is an experience over which no one but ourselves can exercise authority. The experience can be talked about and shared or not, for at times one may need help with deciphering a dream message or symbol. But it is the dreamer's truth and understanding which ultimately must prevail, for the dream experience was one's own, not another person's. Should we ask for help with a dream, the helper needs to be unbiased, nondogmatic, nonauthoritarian, and generally of good and kind intention toward us. Sharing dreams is sharing an intimate part of oneself. It is a wonderful thing to do with the right person or group. Someone who really loves us is a good person to tell a dream to, someone uncaring is not.

When we start to consciously live with and acknowledge the spiritual significance of the dream world, we allow our own genius, our own expertise and hidden deciphering talents to arise and develop. Waiting to be activated according to our own style and type, these talents lay fallow until we use them. Working with a dream is not a purely intellectual or emotional pursuit of truth, for its potential directions and meanings are virtually boundless. Exploring one's dreams and learning about them has nothing to do with formal education or how many degrees one has hanging on a wall. It has everything to do with being an alert human being, open, watching and listening.

We, the Dream

Our dreams deal with the issues, events, and people in the life of the dreamer. Every element has significance, there to be read as a letter from a divine source. What you dream is about who you are—and who you are is about what you dream.

Dreams speak to us about the direction, concerns, and qualities of our life. They are as diverse as people, places, and things are different. A dream is not a randomly created happening of some purely physiological brain activity that we make up into a story line. Such views of dreams belittle the human spirit and its divine source, and keep us limited to that which we have learned to quantify. Can a parent's love for a child be weighed and measured? Can a dream honestly be dismissed merely as a neurological event lacking any other significance?

As with the waking world, the dream world has intention. It has purposes to serve. Nothing is by chance. Our dream is a prod, informing us and urging us on. It has the magnificence and the power to transform our way of looking at and acting in everyday life.

Remembering Dreams

Beliefs form our experience of the world. How we treat our dream life is a reflection of our beliefs. If we do not believe that there are other unseen realities that we are part of, then we may dismiss dreaming as irrelevant or nonsensical, like a moth fluttering around a porch light. Thus, we remove ourselves from a source of spiritual nourishment. So removed, we live without absorbing the divine nutrients that dreams offer.

Some of us don't remember our dreams, others are convinced that they don't dream. The evidence is otherwise. Put simply, we all dream each night. About ninety minutes apart, dream cycles occur during periods of rapid eye movement, blood pressure fluctuations, breathing changes and pulse rate shifts. Many dreams of a longer nature are believed to occur in early morning, prior to waking. This is why, upon waking, our mood may be profoundly influenced by the nature of our dream.

A good night's sleep can help with recollecting what you dreamed when you wake up. In addition, before you go to sleep, tell yourself that you WILL remember your dream in the morning. A pencil and paper on hand by the bed can help so that you can choose to quickly write down the dream before it fades from memory. Don't censor anything in your recollection. Every and any aspect is significant, for within each part of the dream is a piece of the whole. Don't be discouraged if you only remember the tiniest detail, for that detail stands out for a reason. It's up to us to embrace that fragment and own it as a piece of where we are in our life.

The Present Future

Dreams can be prophetic, giving a glimpse of a possible or probable future. This future may be distant or close at hand.

Marie was flying to another state to visit some relatives. It was the birthday party for an eighty-five-year-old cousin, a very special occasion. Other relatives, living some distance away, had also been invited. Marie's attachment was to her niece, Nadine, whom she hadn't seen in a long time. Several days before the party, Nadine called Marie to say she was sorry but she could not attend. Perhaps they would meet at some later date. Marie was disappointed, but accepting. Two days later Marie had this dream:

> I was at a party and there were many people around. It was a fun time. Suddenly I noticed a woman sitting in a corner. She had a veil over her face. I asked others who she was but no one seemed to know. Deciding to find out, I walked over to where she was sitting, bent down and slowly lifted her veil. To my joy and surprise, it was my niece, Nadine. We kissed and hugged. Then I woke up. On waking, I intuitively felt that Nadine would go to the party. I called another relative to tell her, but she pooh-poohed it, saying it was only a dream. I knew differently but kept quiet. The evening before the party, two days after I had the dream, I was getting ready to go to the airport. The phone rang. It was Nadine calling to say that two nights ago, rather late in the evening, she had decided to cancel other plans and come to the birthday celebration. Considering our time difference, it was at about the same time that my dream occurred. When I told her I knew, she did not seem surprised. Neither was I.

Marie was quick to see how a prophecy had been revealed to her. Attuned to the messages sent from the dream world, she noticed the correspondence in her waking life and trusted what she was told. Marie was not special in her ability to read her dreams. She simply understood them as a reality charged with meaning and insight, accepting the revealed messages as one would accept a telegram from a friend. Opening it, reading the message, trusting the intuition, within that moment in her life, knowledge was revealed. She understood that she and Nadine had a special relationship. Continuously in touch despite actual physical distance, their silent contact had been honored in the realm of the invisible. By valuing our dreams and our gut intuition, we receive support and guidance from the unseen world.

A Child Dreams

Children naturally trust. Living open and available to the intelligence of the heart, their dreams often reflect their simple honesty of feeling. Here is one by seven-year-old Sarah who had attended her grandma's funeral the day before. Her mother wept as she put Sarah to bed that night, reading a story with her until the child faded off into sleep. In the morning Sarah said:

> Mommy, I had this dream. I saw a lot of dead people with Grandma. I talked to them. I told them that they could have Grandma but that they couldn't have you.

Sarah did experience a conversation with dead people. Clearly, the child hopes that they will obey her request to leave her mother here in this world. Sarah is in a dialogue with an invisible world, an imagined world in another dimension, but a reality nonetheless.

Entrance into the rich world of images is our birth privilege. It has always been and will always be part of human life. Only recently, in the last two hundred years, has this realm of experience been devalued and called "fantasy" or "illusion."

The innate richness of a dream needs to be understood as the potent oracle it is, understandable on many levels, readable in many ways. To limit a dream's meaning to "wish fulfillment of a sexual nature" is like limiting our vocabulary to just a few words.

A mirror of life, many today are grasping the enlightening nature of the dream phenomenon and implementing fresh meaning into everyday life, as Henry did:

I opened this heavy door leading out of the college and breathed in   ·
the fresh air. It felt good after the hot classroom. Feeling recharged,
I wanted to stay but felt pressured to get home. I had studying to do.
I started to walk toward my car, knowing I had parked it up the hill,
a short distance from the campus. I walked in that direction, looking
for my small, gold-colored sedan. One car stood gleaming in the bold
sunshine, but it wasn't mine. I continued walking, further and further
up the hill. Still no car. Where could it be? I could feel anxiety seep-
ing into me. Suddenly, I was in an unfamiliar place. I stood still. Huge
oak trees were lined up in a row, their massive trunks solidly
grounded in the earth. Houses had lawns flooded with flowers of all
colors—purple, yellow, white, orange, red and pink—a paradise.
But where was my car? How would I get home? Could it have been
stolen? My anxiety was accelerating. Yet, the scene was so compelling
that I stayed and stayed. The next thing I knew was that daylight
was fading and early evening moving in. I became mobilized, wanting
to get home before darkness descended. I started to walk toward my
right, sensing that this was the direction to take. There was my car.
Overjoyed, I unlocked the door and got behind the wheel. Placing my
foot on the gas pedal, I felt something on the heel of my shoe. It was
an apple blossom. I put it in the palm of my hand, remembering that
the apple blossom was a Chinese symbol for peace and beauty.
Inwardly, I made a connection. Then I woke up. But the dream
seemed to stay with me for a long time as I tried to put it all together.

Examining his own dream, Henry realized he was receiving
support for his current direction. He had recently begun a compelling spiritual search. A number of his college courses seemed
vapid and irrelevant. Having started reading about spirituality,
he had become deeply impressed by this new perspective on life.
His car, he now understood, had always been very important to
him. It was his way of getting to where he was going but he had
grown overly dependent on it. Often using it for short distances
when he could just have easily walked, on some level Henry
realized that the car was in control of him. His dream had
revealed to him a message about attachment and enslavement. He
saw in the dream a need to shift his life's values and direction.
Going up a hill, climbing a mountain, his journey was upward,
toward the unknown. Truth and beauty were to replace dependency on outer things. Now climbing the ladder of himself, he

had tapped into the most dependent of all resources, those within us that provide a view and feel for our own direction.

Dreams are markers along the road of life. Often the sign-posts are clear, concrete and obvious. A joyous dream is a joyous dream. We wake up happy, exhilarated and feeling freshly alive. Considering what in the dream put us into this delightful state, we discover something of what happiness means to us. Waking up sad, we learn what of life's offerings saddens us. We can then act on that information and take the necessary action to change a situation, surmount an obstacle, or consider a fresh point of view. Each of us is unique, our dreams and our responses to them are our own. Their truth is what we come to know in our heart and gut to be their meaning, whether we figured it out ourselves or sought interpretive help from a friend.

Expressing where we are, our dreams can involve conflict or harmony, both reflecting and affecting our mood. We can use our dream world of images to change our state or circumstance. Consider the two following dreams. The first is Linda's:

> I am in my office working at the computer. Suddenly I am told the boss wants to see me. Taking what I am working on with me, I enter his office, knowing that he is anxious to see it. He looks at it and begins to shout at me. He tells me I got the instructions all wrong, that I really messed up. He is talking real loud, and I know everyone can hear him for the door is open. Ashamed, angry and humiliated, I start to cry, so embarrassed that I am doing this in front of him. I wake up on a sob.

Linda was angry, moody and upset all day. The dream, she felt, had ruined everything. She could not throw it off, and turned down a date for that night with someone she had just met and found interesting. Linda's belief was that the evening would only turn out to be a disaster. She blamed the dream and chose to feel victimized by it.

Andrea, an elementary school teacher, had the following dream:

> I am marking papers, my children having already been dismissed. It is quiet in the classroom. Suddenly the door is flung open. My principal comes in. He tells me quietly that he has always found me

attractive, that he feels the "vibes" between us. He looks strange, like I hadn't seen him look before. He moves closer to my desk, bends down toward me and starts to say these very personal things. I feel embarrassed and tell him to stop, that this is very inappropriate. He pays me no mind and continues. I feel my anger getting stronger and stronger inside of me. I push my chair away from my desk and stand up. Facing him directly, in my strictest teacher-voice, I tell him that he must leave immediately or I will call Security. His face reddens and he becomes quiet. As he turns to leave, I shout after him, "And shut the door!" He does. I wake up feeling great. I really told him off. The feeling stayed with me all day. I experienced a different side of myself and I like it. Nobody has to take everything. I certainly won't.

Aware that her dream and waking world are replicas of each other, Andrea knows the dream is playing out her life in the present, that the challenges expressed in her sleep world occur in similar fashion in her waking life. The play of the dream world, not different in content from the waking life, is simply presented in the language of images and symbols which can speak in a broad and creative tongue. This image language occurs unhampered by the usual limits of time and space and rational logic where the waking life messages are inscribed.

Wrapped like a present, the feelings and images of a dream reveal our truth to us. Anger, shame, joy, ecstasy, surprise, disappointment, love—all are genuine feelings, presented to us as signposts for our waking life. They confirm where we are or tell us to act. They mercifully alert us to choices we are free to make.

Linda, on the other hand, left herself feeling helpless and victimized. She blamed the dream for her inner state and felt unable to have any dialogue with what had presented itself. She believes she has no choice in the matter. With anger her focus, and unaware that the dream is a cue from the unseen world meant to show her something, she does not move beyond this signpost but stays immersed in it, giving it power over her life. Victimization will most probably keep haunting her just as her dreams, those persistent guides, will most likely continue to send her messages urging change. But only she can make—or not make— decisions to alter the course of matters; for, like a supportive best friend, dreams do not make decisions for us. We make the decision to be active or passive in response to messages from the unseen world.

Choices

Spiritual engagement and growth occur when we learn to make choices that are responsive rather than reactive, or, in other words, intentional rather than mechanical. We then enter into responsibility and true stewardship in the flow of existence.

Linda might have opted to change her dream by working directly with the images that appeared to her. Traditionally, people worked this way with dreams. By reentering her dream, Linda can use her intention to repicture the situation and arrange a different outcome. She can picture her boss speaking to her with respect and decency. Or she can confront him, see herself acting upon a decision to leave her job, inform superiors, empty her office desk, or move on to a more positive and healthful environment. It's her choice of a resolution. Recalling her dream, she can, when awake, with closed eyes, go back into it, see the images, and make any changes she wishes. By re-creating our personal inner images, we help engender support from the universe to elicit change in our life. Encouraging in ourselves this link between the seen and the unseen worlds, we enjoin and mobilize part of the spiritual fabric of being human.

Redoing Our Dream

Jeff, a retired attorney, was having a disquieting, recurrent dream:

> I am in this old building. I walk further inside. There is a coffin placed
> in the center of the room. An old, fairly homely woman is lying in it.
> I look at her and feel a sense of disgust. I turn to leave. Suddenly
> someone appears. He is holding a gun and is about to shoot. It is
> pointing straight at me. I am frozen in fear and wake up, shaken,

but relieved that it is only a dream. But the relief doesn't last long, since I know it will appear again. I wish I could do something about it but what can you do with a dream?

In the past Jeff had always analyzed his dreams, looking for complex interpretations over which he had no control. This time, sitting in an upright yet comfortable position, he re-entered his dream in an alert, waking state, with eyes closed. He simply imagined himself back in the dream. Giving himself permission to bring into his imagery whatever was needed to help himself, he could now make any changes he wished. All decisions were his to make. This is his dream as he re-created it in the waking state:

> I am in this fairly modern-looking building. I walk further inside. There is a long table in the middle of the room. Someone is lying there under a sheet. I can barely see her and so I move nearer. Under the loosely-wrapped covering, I can sense the form of a beautiful woman. I look closely at her. Her face is exquisite, her eyes open, a sea-green, her lips in a smile. I feel aroused and move towards her. Suddenly a man appears, holding a gun. But as he starts to point it directly at me, I swing around in a karate stance and taking him off guard, I kick the gun out of his hand. Frightened, he runs out, the gun lying passively on the floor. I move towards the woman again. She is welcoming. I then recognize her. She is my first sweetheart, my early love.

Fearful of aging, Jeff dreamed of himself as vulnerable and passive. Someone else would have the power, not him. Sexuality was a thing to be shunned. Changing the dream he could now reclaim power, his sense of mastery and competence and his potent sexuality.

Changing the dream, Jeff made changes in his life very quickly. He became a part-time consultant to a law firm and, having been a widower for over ten years, he found a loving woman companion. Jeff was living his present life, now more in accord with his loving nature and his reason for being in the world. His dream had shown him the road to take.

Dreams that occur over and over again suggest that you have work to do. Like someone nagging at you to start or complete a necessary task, the nagging will not stop until you give it your attention. You have only to listen to your inner voice, sent to you from its sacred source, to know the special path which is yours alone. To honor it is to connect to the divine.

On Winged Feet

Your dream is the bearer of a truth, an emissary, the agent sent on the mission in your interest. Tailor-made like a fine fit for an impeccable suit, the dream has been woven for us. It is a custom fit more intimately ours than any clothing could ever be. As with a strong, loving teacher, a dream shows us where we made the wrong turn, where our walk went off the path, where our heart strayed or our thinking erred. These messages are sent in picture form and not through words. What words could sufficiently convey the feelings engendered by falling in love, reading poetry, or watching a sunset? Dreams, our emissaries, send us images for an evolutionary sojourn speaking to the understanding of the heart.

We and our dreams have the most intimate of relationships. During sleep we willingly release a piece of ourselves into another realm. We roam there and bring back the images needed to maintain the balance and harmony necessary for a joyful, meaningful life. The self then re-enters the waking life and the dream's mission is complete. Now having the data needed to make any changes we wish, we simply read the markings, assured that we are being told where we are and where we wish to be.

Embracing the Dream

A dream is a form of intimacy quite different from any other. We need not throw off our dream the moment we awaken any more than we would shrug off a lover, having just tasted the joy of intimacy. We need to give it precious attention, for it is precious time. Moving from dreaming to being fully awake, we are in a state of transition. To savor the dream, we need to appreciate it and embrace its message if at all possible. One way or other, make some effort to remember your dream. Do not feel you must have it in sequence or logical order. The dream itself goes beyond the stringent, overvalued rules of sequential thought. The invisible world operates differently from that of waking life.

When awake we may choose any piece of our dream: a fragment, a beginning, an ending, whatever strikes us as representing us. We can close our eyes again and bring it into awareness. How does it feel? What sensation does it evoke now? Honor whatever stays with you. Trust yourself. Do not allow criticism or judgments to enter. If you wish to fasten the dream more securely into your consciousness, draw a picture of it. We can make an image of the feeling in the dream. What does it look like? If it is love, what is its face, body, form and color? What does sadness look like? Anger, surprise, joy, disappointment? How do they appear? Or, perhaps you would like to write a poem about the dream or fragment of the dream. Short or long, jot down a few lines. Give your dream a voice. You may opt to keep a dream diary, a tracing of your journey. Reading it will be like looking at a picture album, its continuously changing images reflecting the kaleidoscope of your life.

A Nightmare of Compassion

Nightmares, upsetting as they may be, also have a purpose. They can be a warning that a problem exists, or they can be signs of a conflict between the dreamer and her sacred itinerary. Sent as a spiritual alarm, as with all alarms, they come to alert the dreamer that something is askew. It may not seem apparent. Listen to Jane's dream:

> I am running down the street. Suddenly this horrible thing is chasing me. I do not know what it looks like, whether it is human or beast, but I know I have to get away or it will kill me. It is catching up on me. I scream out but no one hears me. I know I will surely die and wake up with a pounding heart and headache.

Awake, Jane questions her waking life. She thinks, *Everything is O.K. I like my job and my husband and I are doing just fine. If it wasn't for this miserable nightmare, life would be good.* A short time later, it dawns on her: *The truth is, I'm miserable in my marriage. He drinks and then becomes verbally abusive and sometimes even attempts to strike me, but I dodge in time. He gets so ugly during those times. I'm scared to death.*

As can be plainly seen, there are no contradictions between dream and waking life. When Jane became aware of the correlation between her two worlds, she was able to make new decisions. Understanding the urgency of her dream message, she was forced to confront a lopsided life. She found the strength to take the necessary action to restore harmony and balance to her existence. Her dream world had sent mirror images functioning as catalysts in a spiritual process of realignment. It shattered denial and restored her spirit on its journey.

Dreams are concrete. They are about what is going on in your life. Like the dinner bell, the message is loud and clear. We need only listen. Tamar listened sensitively to her own dream:

> I am standing on a narrow bridge above a body of water. My hus-
> band is with me. I cannot go down and so I call out "Help us" to
> anyone who might be there. Someone hears and comes to help, but
> tells me that my husband is already safely on shore, that he has man-
> aged to come down. I am thinking to myself in the dream that this is
> just like him, his usual behavior.

Tamar is reading her life situation as it is, in the form of a poetic, dramatized set of images. After many years of marriage, she is contemplating divorce. Her husband's self-centeredness seemed to always be getting in the way of a real partnership, her understanding of marriage. However, since they had been talking with some degree of success most recently, she had decided to try staying together a bit longer. Her dreams will continue to instruct in the decisions to be made.

Some dreams, while clear in their message to the dreamer, raise a serious concern about an important question in one's life. It is up to each person whether to act on the message or not. This challenge occurred in the dream and waking life of Mollie:

> I am near a college where I study. I go to park my car. A man
> approaches me and tells me I have to get insurance to park it. I ask
> how much and he says, $6,000. I am furious and tell him that this is

a great deal for parking for an hour. But, he insists and so I pay it.
I am very angry and then I wake up.

Mollie explained to a friend that she was seeing a therapist
"to get some direction in life, but I am not getting any from the
process with this person." Her anger, she knew, was directed at
this but she was staying with her therapist hoping that she could
somehow work it out. While still with this therapist, she does
not believe she is getting anything from the process. Though feeling trapped by her therapist's power over her, her dreams
continue to guide her, sending messages urging her to listen to her
own voice. It is her choice to heed or ignore them.

Life Transitions

Affected by the natural changes in the body that come with
aging, we grapple with the newness of transformation. While wisdom, humanity, and compassion are the hallmarks of spiritual
ripening, not our calendar age, it sometimes takes dreams to
reveal our true feelings about physical aging, not a truth easily
touched. We are culturally disadvantaged concerning aging, the
focus these days being more on the physical changes than
the deeper questions of the life of spirit. After all, we are bom-
barded by endless antiaging messages and merchandising to gloss
over and demean a profound truth of our journey. In spite of
physical changes, our external power in the world can give way
to an ennoblement of the inner life. Thus, while for some per-
sons aging is a loss of power and an inability to accept a more
tranquil, laid-back position, for others it presents no problem—
only choice.

John was a well-known painter, internationally famous for
his sensuous portraits of nudes. Now aged seventy-five, he had
been suffering from a number of chronic, if not debilitating,
ailments. His work had slowed down. This is his dream:

I am walking along a shoreline. It is a beautiful, bright, and sunny day
and I am feeling buoyantly alive. Suddenly something is washed

ashore, a wave pulling it in. I walk over to see what it is. It is three mermaids, extremely beautiful. But they are dead. I stand there frozen. Such beauty and so dead. I wonder how that can be. Transfixed, I stand there and stare and stare. Then I hear voices calling to me. They are the voices of friends of mine calling me to join them. But I cannot go, cannot leave this scene of beauty and death.

Comfortable with his intuition, John was aware of what the dream meant to him. From his life as a painter, he had learned that it takes a combination of three elements to create an artistic possibility in a painting: form, color, and texture. This, he felt, was keenly reflective of his current life. Living with the beauty essential to his life, he could not bear to give it up. Nor could he deny the frailties besieging him. He saw three elements in his waking life. He had passion for the beautiful, fear of encroaching illness, and a deep love of life. He needed to find a way to connect to his current possibilities. He made a decision. He would return to painting, doing it for short periods each day. In between, he would rest when he had to. His passion for esthetics, for beauty, need not be relinquished. Death would wait. Life was now. John's new paintings are more powerful and sensitive than ever, and his health, although not perfect, is no longer an overwhelming problem in his life.

Emanuel, a surgeon of many years, now only had a partial medical practice. He dreamt:

I was in uniform with a regiment. There were many men around and the feel of destruction. A cannon was nearby. I could have a lot of power to shoot. Suddenly the "enemy" approached. I realized they were only men like everyone else and I did not even know them. Why would I shoot them? I decided not to and left the scene.

Emanuel understood the dream as a message. This is how he expressed it:

I have my own power to do what I wish. I am getting older and am semiretired from my profession as a medical doctor. Still, I have power but it is the power to make choices and experience each day more deeply. I can now use it in the most beneficial way. It doesn't have to be a destructive experience or a loss.

For Emanuel, this was a moment of renewal and spiritual clarity that changed his life.

Dreams of death in various forms have been noted throughout history. Spiritual traditions universally consider a dream of the dead to be directly related to sacred powers, a solid connection to the divine. When someone has this type of dream, she feels a particular intensity. She reports a real experience of a deceased person being there, in the dream. It is so real that sometimes people say it was less like a dream and more like a visitation that one could imagine occurring in the waking state—hearing, seeing, and even touching the person, as though the dreamer were not sleeping at all.

A typical example follows. The dreamer is a woman in her fifties whose sister, twenty years her senior to whom she had been very close, had recently passed away:

> It was a short dream but, on the other hand, it seemed to go on forever, it was that powerful. I was coming into a room and out of the corner of my eye, I could see my sister, Judith. Her face was shining, almost aglow. She was lying on a couch but her face was lit up. It radiated love. I was so moved and felt such intense love inside of me that I could not move. I felt caught in the moment. I just stood in the room and stared at her. I wanted her to know of my deep yearnings for her, how I missed her and how important she had been to me all my life. She did not move or speak but I felt she understood. Then I left. But the feelings in the dream stayed even after waking. They were so powerful. I knew we had really, in truth, made this incredible connection. Just like we had in life.

A dream of someone who died but was once close to us can be a way of final closure. Dorie said good-bye for the last time in her dream:

> Feeling so alone after my husband's death and longing deep down inside to speak to him and see him once again, my prayers were answered. I woke up with tears in my eyes and an overwhelming feeling of contentment in my heart for that night he came to me in a dream that felt so true and real. He was crawling on his knees through what looked like an open tunnel. His face was bright as if reborn. His arms were reaching out to me as though he wanted to touch my hands. I remember standing still, not knowing what to do. I awoke

feeling happy and sad at the same time. This dream I will carry with me for as long as I live for I feel I was able to see him one last time. I needed to.

Dorie had come home from work to find her husband dead from a drug overdose. Never having had time to say good-bye, her dream now granted her that opportunity. The realms that reveal themselves in dreams are full of the mysteries of existence. They remind us of our spirit, offering a direct line to a form of practical transcendence where all things are possible.

A Confirmation

The spiritual journey is about the truth that we believe to be true. While never closing ourselves off from a new perspective, we learn to receive our validation not from others, but from inside our own heart. We are called upon to accept our own challenge, our own path, and receive feedback from the universe through the experiences of waking life and dreams. The dream world sometimes sends messages of correction, but it also can confirm that we are on the right track. Consider this dream that came to Lawrence, a health professional and a well-respected spiritual leader in his community:

I was in the room of a house. I knew it was my house but nothing felt familiar. All of a sudden, I found myself being lifted up off the ground by an irresistible force. I began flying. I was still in a standing position but gently flying through the room of the house. I became aware of a force and a presence lifting me and I felt something underneath my right arm. I shifted my gaze to the right where, out of the corner of my eye, I realized there was a brown, furry creature that was lifting me. I didn't want to look too closely because I felt some fear about this creature. But the creature said to me very reassuringly, "Don't be afraid. I'm your friend." The sensation of levitating through the house was absolutely exhilarating. Eventually we sailed through an open door and landed on a pier or a dock. There was water to one side, like the ocean or some other body of water. A lot of my friends were standing on the dock. The creature gently set me down there. It came out from underneath my arm and I realized that it had become a white goose. It then said something like, "My job is over," and gave me some kind of a warm farewell. It spread its wings in order to stretch. As it unfurled its wings, it became obvious that parts of its wings were brightly colored in blue, yellow, and red—the primary colors.

Lawrence had an intuitive sense of what his dream meant:

My feeling is that the dream is about freedom, power and change, about letting go toward the freedom, the wildness inside myself. I woke up feeling privileged to have had this dream, very happy that I got to fly. It felt like an out-of-body experience. I had this physical sensation of leaving my body. The whole dream was very exciting.

He also told about something that happened the next day:

Today a brochure came that my wife and I had sent away for about a rental for summer in North Carolina. There were many cottages advertised, but the one that struck us the most is called "The Snow Goose," just like the goose in my dream. And the three colors would be the three of us going there—my wife, myself, and our daughter.

Lawrence welcomed his dream of flying as a sign of spiritual freedom, a message of awakening to a more evolved level of understanding. It coincided with his feelings in waking life and confirmed his inner sense.

Whether a dream is of flying or standing still, it is our most precious inner voice addressing us, guiding us on the royal road of living toward the sacred portable now.

Chapter 6

THE BODY AS KNOWLEDGE

We enter this world a nearly translucent physical form. Our birth is recorded as the time and place when the body first emerged, distinct and independent from our mother's womb. As time goes by, physical growth, learning, coordination, mobility, balance, agility, and eventually talking become testimonies to the miracle of creation. Our senses, alive, active and available, soak in impressions and radiate life. In undivided innocence, we have lived in the present, in the vibrancy of the sacred portable now.

Our passage into adulthood and the arena of free will is unique to each of us. Individual strengths and weaknesses naturally and inevitably unfold and present themselves. With such profound growth, however, there is the problem of becoming hardened and less available to the subtler life energies that inform existence and constitute the life of the spirit. The buoyancy, malleability, sensitivity, and presence that characterize the early years form into a more tightly defined being that we come to call "myself," and with which we meet an intricate world. In the process, we become increasingly complex, more experienced, more what we call "grown up"; but the downside is that in many ways we get complicated and less sensitive to many things. We cut ourselves off from a large part of our birth privilege by building thoughts and attitudes about ourselves far in excess of our real need. We learn to live more in our heads and our moodiness, severely compromising a direct experience of the world of sensation-perception, feeling the body, experiencing the sensations of life. For many of us, varieties of sensory experience that were once part of our early youth have become mostly a matter of what feels good, or what doesn't feel good, what I like and what I don't like.

Although we are physically feeling creatures, sensation has not been well incorporated into our complex culture. We are not generally taught to value sensory alertness. Hence, it suffers disuse, rendering it less than the attentive servant it was designed to be. Feeling comfortable or feeling nothing at all, we are more or less satisfied to live with a minimum of sensory experience.

Most thrill-seeking is a desperate attempt to wake up sensation, to feel physically alive. Our physical sensation is more often than not experienced as something separate, a part of ourselves we might be lucky enough to meet in a stretch class, while having a massage, or during the first few moments of an inspiring spring after a long cold winter.

Feeling something uncomfortably wet or hot with a hand, we experience the sensation of touch, the life of the skin and nerves. But otherwise, it is rare to feel what we touch. This same limitation holds true for all of our senses. Our attention is pulled to our sensations like a wake-up call, but rarely do we choose to live in sensation, that garden we dwelt in as a child.

This present moment contains the seed for recovering some of our own lost spiritual authority by consciously reconnecting to our ability to physically sense ourselves and the world. We can move beyond a limited reaction like "This feels good" or "This feels bad" into a larger and spiritually beneficial field of sensory awareness. What often distinguishes the talker from the person who actually walks the spiritual journey is the participation and awareness of sensation.

Every living organism is gifted with its own fullness of perception, each in accordance with its design, each in keeping with the gifts that distinguish its being. A frog has an essential "frogness," alive in the world as only a frog can be. It senses its own corporeality and the world from the point of view of a frog. We as human beings have an essential humanness, alive in the world as only humans can be, sensing ourselves and the world from the human point of view. Unfortunately, our humanness is often defined by our thoughts and emotions alone. Our mind abstracts life and removes it from the wholeness of experience. The human intellectuality builds thoughts, concepts, and memories, useful in some ways but spiritually devastating if overused or misapplied. Useless mental and emotional obstacles are easily constructed at a swift and alarming rate, pushing us farther into the past that was or future that isn't here. It is true to our habit to consume the meal of the moment with little awareness and presence of being. Yet this very same food, served each moment of our life, beckons us every minute to participate in the sacred now.

The Breath of Life

Anytime is a good time to realize that we are breathing. Imagine a newspaper reporter telephoning to inquire, "We would like to ask your opinion. Do you think you are breathing right now?" Chances are, we would respond affirmatively, confident that we are alive. But in order to truly answer the question authoritatively, from the moment, in order to be aware that we are in fact breathing, we need to actually sense or experience the in-and-out of the breathing cycle.

Awareness of breathing is a simple yet profound means of reorienting the whole organism toward spirit. Most traditions equate breath and spirit. Just as the first cry of a newborn marks our presence here on earth, the final breath we take is acknowledged as the moment when the spirit departs the body and moves on into another mystery.

Awareness of the breathing cycle is easy to do. It can be done anywhere, at any time. However, we recommend that you not try any of these methods while driving a car or doing any other activity which could be physically dangerous to oneself or others. We are experimenting with awareness, and it needs to be done in completely safe settings.

Here's one way to connect to the breath. Put down this book for a moment. If you need to, close your eyes, but it is not necessary. Accept where you are, how you are. Pick a point on your body, the chest, the ribs or the belly—a place where the body moves when you breathe. For example, if you choose your belly, notice that it gets bigger, reaches a point of expansion and then relaxes back toward the body. When the belly expands, we are breathing in. When the belly deflates, we are breathing out. Since our mind easily wanders, it might be helpful to say to yourself "breathing in" and then "breathing out" to reinforce the awareness on the breath. If the awareness of the breath goes away, simply notice the thoughts rattling on in your head. They are just passing thoughts. Don't be hostile to them, just notice them, as you would notice the voices of children playing outside. Bring the attention back to the in-and-out of the breathing. If you do this, even for a minute, you have shifted your attention to a sacred space, where momentary awareness deepens.

Whenever possible, it is always good to sit upright, but the most important thing is to attend to the breathing. Don't change the breathing, simply be with it and appreciate it.

Once we understand this shift of focus to the breath, we can apply it in many life situations. Simple focus on the breathing can be practiced while walking, sitting, standing, or even lying down.

Breathing accompanies us throughout our life, and we can observe our breathing anywhere, whether moving about or doing a simple activity like hanging up a jacket or standing on a train platform. We need not do anything more complicated than just witnessing and appreciating the natural rhythm of breathing. It is a private affair. No one else need notice your shift of focus. Even if you find yourself slouching in a lazy position on a couch, laughing with some friends and eating ice cream, you can still practice bringing awareness to this moment of breathing. In this approach, we are not trying to improve anything, we're simply trying to be aware. (It sounds strange, but often it is the simplest possibilities that we avoid taking advantage of.)

It is not necessary to create the right atmosphere, sit the right way or necessarily change the setting one is in, although if it is possible to close the door, dim the lights, take off your shoes and adjust your sitting posture for optimum balance and poise, that would be all for the good. Simple breathing awareness, done intermittently for small moments throughout the day, is a tangible spiritual entry point. It never need disrupt one's responsibilities to the outer world. But the simplicity of the exercise begins to take on a life of its own as we develop skill at doing it.

We take a giant step in practical spiritual work when we experience the connection between simple awareness of the breath and the life of spirit.

Being Breathed

We don't own our life, although we are called upon to face it, embrace it, live it and take responsibility for it. Owning only that which cannot be taken from us, it might be more helpful to think of our lifetime as a loan. Often we are more conscious and careful about things we borrow from others than the things we own. When we borrow money from someone, we are obliged to pay it back. Spiritually, we have been given the gift of life, but it is a gift on loan.

"We" are not breathing. We are "being breathed." The creative source of the universe gives us a life that is sustained by the breath. We are a vessel, a receptacle for life and the force that fills us is this ever-expanding and -contracting respiration. In fact, the word *respiration* contains the root of the word *spirit*.

Stopping for a moment in the middle of a busy day, returning to the recognition that we are being breathed, that our life is sustained in spite of ourselves, we come back to the present, simplified as a person and less ego-centered. We sense our place in the vastness of creation. If only for a moment or two, we are attuned to a location within ourselves where healthy humility is born anew.

Humility is an extraordinary impulse. It gives rise to a profound wish of service to evolution and life. It engenders in us a deep yearning to act on the side of those forces within ourselves and the world that contribute to our own and the collective well-being.

When we choose to consciously participate in a moment, we notice the inhalation and the exhalation, quietly sensing the mystery of being breathed. If necessary, we can say to ourselves, "I am being breathed." A taste of this experience allows our perception to expand and teaches us the universal quality of being humble and in service to the divine.

Each of us has a different kind of a day, owing to our individual life conditions. Finding the moments—for a half minute or more—when you can experience yourself being breathed may be transformational on many levels. Let your experience be your guide.

Holy Breathing

It is not by chance that *wholeness* and *holiness* sound alike. They speak to a paradigm of unity, a totality containing the many. When we do something in a whole way, with all of ourselves fully attentive, we are connecting to the truth of the divine, for the sacred is also one. A whole movement in our own consciousness corresponds to this unifying principle, and the creation of which we are a part suddenly illuminates our experience.

Another way to shift from the part to the whole is by being aware of the totality of breathing. Most of the time we experience the breathing as happening in the nose, the mouth, the torso, the chest or the belly. But our skin, the largest organ in the body, also takes in and expels air.

Haven't we all stood in amazement watching the open feeling of life energy pulsing through the newborn child? We stand as if magnetized by the rhythm of expansion and contraction that permeates the infant's existence. His breathing is occurring everywhere, from his head to his feet. Even the earlobes are not left out! What we are experiencing in the baby, we have all felt too, but have forgotten it in ourselves.

To reconnect to this whole-body breathing we need only change our attention, not our breath. It is as if we are remembering our porosity, our translucency, the subtler aspects of our form. The porousness of the skin is the quality that keeps us connected to the outside world while allowing us to be individual and unique in shape and size.

We allow the whole body to breathe, right down to our fingertips and toes, each inhalation and exhalation another opportunity to sense our protoplasmic nature, our malleability. We physically feel our interconnectedness with the atmosphere around us and perhaps beyond us, to truly experience the whole-ness—the holiness—of which our organism is a part. Our solidity gives way to a pulsating presence, a completeness of experience linking us to everything that lives and breathes.

Roosting, Rising, and Roaming

Simply stated, sometimes we are sitting, sometimes we are stand-ing, and sometimes we are walking. Universal and timeless, this fact of life is rarely appreciated for its spiritual significance. In our language, we speak of sitting still, standing upright, and walk-ing our path. In museums we see portraits and paintings of people standing, statues of people sitting, and decorative motifs painted on ancient urns of people walking around an entire vase. These three different uses of the body are spiritual themes con-sistently repeated but rarely explored.

Sitting in Sitting

When sitting in a chair, something most of us do many times or hours a day, we get our physical sense of grounding from our con-tact with the seat of the chair. We are temporarily "staying put" by limiting our location to one place. Sitting shows up as part of the natural rhythm of everyday life. Certain activities seem to lend themselves to sitting simply because we don't need to move around a room to do them, or else the activity is simply not par-ticularly portable. When we sit we somewhat simplify, but by no means eliminate, our need for physical balance. Sitting is also often associated with giving our legs a break, and naturally points us in the general direction of the quality of stillness. As a result, it is analogous to the spiritual quality of receptivity or being, more than the equally important quality of action or doing. In spiritual work, we are learning to discern but not judge.

Let's say you are sitting at a table in an informal restaurant. Your friend has gotten up and gone to the lavatory, or perhaps it is a fast-food restaurant and they are still on line getting their food. So there is a wait. Our circumstances have given us a moment with ourselves. The conscious recognition that we are sitting is Creation reminding us that we can open up to the receptive quality within, the easy acceptance of this moment as and where we find ourselves. Because I am sitting, I can become this event, this condition, allowing no other requirement to enter the moment. If a thought comes, I let it go. I accept the receptive sitting position the body is in and honor the moment with awareness, allowing the inner condition to correspond to the outward facts. The ordinary is changed into a sacred act of simplicity, for we allow fuller presence and richer experience to arise through attentiveness to the now. I simply sit because the moment I am in is about the act of sitting. So it becomes an active, alert quiescence. I become the embodiment and the mentality of sitting. In that moment, I am living out and becoming an archetype of life, the sitting human. It may sound humorous or even bizarre to think of oneself as an archetype, connected to any person in the world who has ever experienced sitting, but we are, nevertheless. Transcending time-bound thinking, we are participating in a mindful action of expanded consciousness within the physical truth that life has brought us.

Taking a Stand

Standing upright is the act of balancing oneself between heaven and earth. It is an extraordinarily complex event that the lucky are blessed to discover. Standing in daily living, waiting in lines, getting up from a chair, preparing to cross a street, washing some dishes, buying a ticket at the cinema—these and other ordinary activities await our fuller, more active interest to be fully appreciated. The miracle of balance in the full upright is a human specialty, a gift of creation that expresses our uniquely human sensitivities. Adaptability, availability, flexibility, poise, and vulnerability are reflected in the balancing act of the upright position. It is a living expression of our spiritual possibilities and can teach us much about the necessary qualities that inform an open and available state.

The standing position requires an alert condition that shuns rigidity. Standing with active yet easeful poise requires intelligence, interest, and conscious intent if it is to feed our aspirations toward spirit. As creatures of habit, there are conditioned and automatic ways we stand that we have become accustomed to. We feel a certain amount of comfort and temporary ease when we succumb to an addiction, even though in the longer run we are profoundly hurting ourselves and going against our spiritual purpose of promoting consciousness on earth. Spiritually, it can be very useful to get to know these habitual choices we make in the upright stance. They mirror our inner states, our personal beliefs about ourselves and the world. Very often they tell us we are cut off from a sense of balance within our deeper self.

There are many systems and theories about posture, alignment, and movement. It is not our aim here to burden the reader with many details and exercises that help to improve our relationship to standing. What is important, however, is that the standing position be acknowledged and felt by being aware.

In our culture, standing tall is erroneously associated with the military posture: holding oneself neck back, chest up, legs taut, and so on. Nothing could be further from the happiness of a poise and balance that informs a healthful uprightness. We need to experiment and feel into our balance, allowing for the right and necessary support to occur without holding on and freezing any parts of the body. It is important to note that standing without moving a leg here or a foot there is not our average way in the world. However, for presence and awareness, working with calming down our impulse to shift can be a helpful demand. It places us in a more conscious and present inner condition. There is no judgment in all of this. We can take it as an experiment or a study that we undertake for the sake of finding out more about ourselves and our awareness in a moment. Any inner activity that engenders greater consciousness brings us closer to spirit.

See how it feels when you place your feet straight ahead instead of turned out. Notice how it impacts on the equation of balance. Very subtly, we can shift our weight a little forward, a little back, experiencing the changing sensation. Balancing the body ever so slightly forward, we find the ground with the soles of our feet, the weight centered directly over the arch, between the heel and the toes. Allow the head to lighten and float upward while the neck is gently, imperceptibly finding its freedom to be long, easy, and gently supported. Don't force anything. It's a waste of time to apply force where quiet perception is called for. Forcefulness hinders rather than helps one to understand the moment. Check the weight over the whole foot, the pelvis and the spine, including the neck and the head. Inwardly acknowledge that the head stands available for movement, balancing delicately on top of the spine. The neck doesn't rigidify the head and the weight of the poising head need not compress the neck and immobilize it. Feel the spine and pelvis easily, fluidly, balancing on the legs, and the legs standing freely on top of the ankles, the arches alive and buoyant. Let your arms hang freely, but if you are carrying something, just use these suggestions to feel into being more sensitive to balance, rather than bracing ourselves in an off-centered way. Experiment and discover!

Remember, our concern is not self-improvement or vanity, but rather, perception, awareness, and openness. Encouraging openness in the body is a spiritually beneficial practice that enhances our connection to the sacred. One need not do this "correctly" in order to be involved with increased consciousness.

Waiting for a bus, standing in line at the market or waiting to go into a bathroom during intermission at the theater becomes another chance to practice awareness. The usual frustrations of waiting and standing can be transformed into serious spiritual opportunity, a return to our pursuit of a more conscious, present existence grounded in respect for the sacred element in living.

To Walk the Earth

The spiritual journey is within the stream of life whenever we find it, in whatever we are doing. As an artful sojourn, it is a work in process, discovered in the continuous flow of activity informed by consciousness. Our spiritual needs cleave to the processes we are engaged in as we live life. Results are not nearly as important to focus on. When we cross a street, our practical intelligence tells us that it is getting to the other side that matters the most. The spirit tells us it is the process of getting across that matters. They both matter, but our focus here is on process.

Tending to rush around as we do, we drag ourselves through space, our eyes on getting things done, arriving at where we are going. Reacting rather than responding to life's needs, we usually allow the outer demand to lead us around by the nose. Most of us move in patterns and attitudes stored in ourselves that were formed in the past and endlessly repeat themselves in the present. This very moment—the now—eludes us in part because our anxieties about the future and our memorized past are stored in how we walk our journey. There is no attitude or conception in the mind that doesn't have a corresponding freedom or restriction in the physical body.

The experience of walking can be sensed or felt. Sensing with the body is like tasting or smelling. It is the "taste" the body has of itself. This can include experiencing our stature, our gait, the internal jiggles the body makes when we stride and reach the floor, the stiffness we feel as well as the freedoms we experience in different parts of the body. Imagine walking across a room with a blindfold on. Attuned to what you sense with each step, each feel for balance or safety, your sensation alert, you become more animal, connected to the instinctual part of motion. Under these circumstances, deprived of sight, the sensation is thrust to the forefront of your awareness. This is the arena of bodily aware-ness that can enlighten any situation in life. You can, at will, access this arena and infuse a moment with newness, reaffirming your presence in the sacred now.

Walking affords one with a moment to oneself, a time and a place to return to a simple presence, beyond thinking and worrying, into the realm of the body. A simple walk from one point to another can be a moment of regaining an uncomplicated and more spiritually aligned presence. All we need is to apply our ability to choose to place our attention on sensation when we walk.

Often, we walk the same sidewalk, path, hallway, shortcut or driveway over and over again. This type of repetition in life is inevitable and invaluable. It can be raised to a level of profound practice, if we so choose. A long corridor in an office, traversed six times a day, can actually become a reminder that life is something sacred, that we are not just mechanical beings. We turn within such a moment to a practice of awareness of walking, a spiritual effort to consciously, intentionally encounter the present. Slowing down or speeding up might be useful, but they are not necessary components of this study. Befriending our unique manner of walking by sensing it and experiencing its nuance, is a form of self-knowledge that can not be learned through books, discussions, or thinking. A moment of the purposeful embrace of the sensation of walking ushers us into the stream of our spiritual possibility.

Tying a Shoe, Turning a Doorknob

Watch a young child tie his shoe, one who has just mastered the skill. Each intentional meander of the shoestring, every movement of the arms and fingers unfolding, like a mystery drama revealing its intricacies. A moment full of intense interest, concentration, presence of mind and presence in the body, the process is everything and the child gives it his all.

The key word here is *mystery*. When we travel through life with a "been there, done that" attitude (to use the vernacular), the light of the spirit becomes obscured. The sacredness of life becomes overcast with clouds of familiarity. As the saying goes, familiarity breeds contempt. Wishing for an experience of life that is in the divinity of the present, we are called upon to do battle with complacency and inattention.

There is nothing in our way to prevent us from experiencing the mystery of tying our shoe, threading a needle, opening up a wrapped stick of gum, turning a doorknob, using a can opener, passing the salt and pepper at dinner, or even brushing our teeth. From the point of view of the task, it matters very little if we attend to what we are doing with fullness of heart, mind and body. But from a spiritual perspective, it probably matters much more than reading this book.

Let us return to tying a shoe. It is a complete and singular process, that by analogy contains the possibility of our own completeness and singularity. Furthermore, it is a microcosm of all creation and mirrors its intricacies and oneness. We can notice, then, that the small details of our life contain spiritual correspondence. Seeing our simple life activities as separate, fragmented aspects of living cut off from the quest for the sacred never helps us. Instead, what we need is to interact with the larger picture, the interconnectedness of all things. We do this superficially, by acknowledging this truth through an idea; but we make the possibility real by taking inner action along with the outer activity. It is through the deed of activating our intention and awareness in a specific direction that we participate spiritually in the mundane world.

The action we take is an active shift of the attention toward witnessing and sensation. We already know how to tie a shoe. Registered in the synapses of our brain and within the cellular memories of our muscles, it is a rote skill so well known that it avoids our full participation and appreciation. By feeling into the activity of tying a shoe, including awareness of the whole body, we become alive to a mystery. Witnessing and fully experiencing the small movements of the fingers and the hand, being with the sense of touch and allowing the deftness of the hand–eye coordination to be noticed and felt, the miraculous that is at play in everything for a moment sounds its elusive note. Mystery becomes an experience, as we consciously experience and appreciate the gift of dexterity. We engage a small action in a big way, leaving behind the stories and dramas we build with the mind, and focus our attention on the detail of the moment. Like a master artisan, we fully participate and serve the craft of daily living.

Many of us are waiting for the conditions of life to be "just right" or maximally convenient to practice deepening within ordinary life. There is really no need to delay, and there is no time to waste. Peeling an orange with presence has as much magical spiritual possibility as a well constructed "quiet time" scenario. Our difficulty is in what we believe is possible and what effort we are willing to make to be alive and attentive. Sense the hand grasping a doorknob as you turn it, and life returns to the present tense. Through repetition of this awareness, the doorknob becomes a friendly wake-up call when we have forgotten the sacred component in our existence. We receive back only as much as we put in. The interest and the effort are the two necessary elements of all spiritual discipline.

Honest Hunger

Eating is one of our biggest cultural preoccupations. Profitable businesses flourish based on a widespread interest in nutrition, health, social responsibility, pleasure, convenience, time management, weight-loss, weight-gain, vanity, and even immortality. Books, seminars, experts, research, theories, television programs, products, cooking machines, diets, ancient cuisine, organic vegetables, new high-protein grains from antiquity, even designer mushrooms from European cellars fascinate our pliable palates and searching (though suggestible) minds. Nevertheless, despite all the abstract thoughts we have about food, we find ourselves two, three or four times daily seated at a table, standing at a deli counter or positioned on a bench near where we work, nourishing the animal that we are.

Luckily, our animal nature demands that we eat. If the physical need for food was not translated into a desire to eat, we might tend to forget and disregard the organism's basic need for fuel. Our desire to eat, therefore, is a vital sign of life, a benefactor and ally on the spiritual journey. A continuous reminder of our physical, earthbound nature, it is a demonstration of our two-edged sword of strength and vulnerability. When we are hungry, we want food. When we have satisfied the need to eat, the attention is freed to seek nutrients from other parts of life.

There are numerous ways of bringing awareness into the act of eating. One of the simplest ways is to tune into the gut sense and question whether the body is truly hungry or not. Often assuming that wanting to eat is in fact genuine hunger, we deprive ourselves of the cellular consciousness which is purely of the body. There is a part of the brain that was designed to tell us that we require bodily nourishment at this moment. The hypothalamus gives a signal that in many of us still functions, but in most of us is poorly received or overridden by years of out-of-balance eating habits. We can barely hear its faint, honest message. Deep down, we know whether our desire to eat is truly from the cells or else from emotional need or enslavement to schedule.

Taking notice of the difference between genuine physical need and mere want is an important enlargement of self-knowledge, one of the most important tools that our spirit has. In addition, attuning to the true bodily need, rather than only the want, we improve the quality of our life and health. We are not passing judgment here or saying what is the correct way to approach eating. Again, these are suggestions to be experimented with if they ring true.

Our discernments are for us to make and ours to act upon alone. If we see that we are eating out of habit, emotional need or addiction, the important thing might be to see and live that truth, to experience that inner contradiction in the present. This kind of protective eating is formed from beliefs keeping unnecessary residues of the past alive. It is a form of living in the past, obscuring the present. It is distant from the truth of the moment, where the sensations that are connected to the true physiological needs of the body reside. However, if you dwell in that contradiction long enough, there will probably be consequences or stronger messages that might compel you to act on what you know. That is the longer, more painful way, a form of learning by the method of "hard knocks." The less painful way is to listen, learn, and act upon what the body is telling us the moment we notice. Then our intention is acting from the subtler feedback system built into creation rather than waiting for the presence of a louder message, a greater challenge or a health emergency. (An example of a louder message might be waking up one day and finding none of your clothes fit, due to significant weight gain.)

The universe is always giving us messages that keep us on a path aligned with the one creation of which we are a part. Our job is to be scrupulously truthful with ourselves and genuinely interested in a spiritually engaged existence. We are asked to respond to this oneness, which is what responsibility—the ability to respond—is all about. Distinguishing true hunger from other forms of craving is an excellent practice to synchronize our awareness with the present.

Being Eating

Eating can be done attentively or inattentively. Either we have made the choice to be present with our process of eating or we haven't. We need to learn to be inwardly sincere, if we wish honestly to "walk our talk." Living in the gift of the moment, the privilege of receiving food from the universe is a sacred act. It is a pleasurable, inherently satisfying event that easily lends itself to a deepening of spiritual presence. As a built-in ritual of existence, it gives us an engaging opportunity to live more fully in the moment a few times each day.

Feeling the movements of the body, being with the tastes and textures of the food we eat, we can anchor in the world of sensation. Awareness is not "about" eating, but rather it is pure physical experience. A process overseen by our larger intelligence, but part of our instinctual nature, it is a series of alive, real moments. There is the moment when we put the fork into a piece of food or the sensation of moving the arm, of holding the fork, feeling the fork going into the food, lifting the fork. There are processes such as chewing, tasting, and swallowing. The possibilities for enlarging our awareness are as endless as our consciousness. Tasting has many levels, qualities, and details that can be experienced by taking the initiative to go against our habit. Tending to gloss over the process, we can instead direct the attention to fully participate in and notice the different parts of the activity. We have crunches to hear and jaw movements to feel. We have plates to lift, wrappers to unwrap, smells to smell and tastes to explore. It is a rich and fertile field of experience. Most of the time we miss ninety-nine percent of it because we basically don't make it important. Rather, we often live in real or imagined time constraints that cause us to rush through the meal. In fact, there is usually plenty of time and space in our eating to be aware. We simply need to value and accept the spiritual challenge and benefits of conscious eating and attend to it to the best of our ability. Even if we are apparently stuck eating in a short moment, due, let us say, to a madcap schedule, the attention can go at an increased speed, and experience what it is able to. It is there to be directed and brought to the moment, brief and speedy though may be the circumstances. It takes strong initiative on our part, but the effort is well spent and can only be spiritually beneficial. But the truth is, there is usually enough time to slow down a little bit and engage ourselves more fully in the moment.

Imagine somebody making this offer: "Extend the time you spend eating each meal by at least four minutes. Be present with the food and the process of eating, significantly more so and more often than is your habit. Each time you consume a meal in this new manner, you will receive $250 per meal. Otherwise, you will receive nothing." Only the very rare and probably very wealthy person would not find a way to eat a bit less frenetically, more consciously, in equal measure.

Valuing our eating for its priceless spiritual importance, to do what we intuitively understand is part of our evolutionary task, is to become more awake to the sacred portable now.

Gratitude as Food

Nothing is as simple as inwardly expressing gratitude for a gift. In our supermarket culture we live in a mirage of abundance, believing that the availability of food is a permanent condition. Living in a world of haves and have-nots, of affluence and poverty, we tend to take the forces that sustain us for granted. Globally,

Chapter 7

━━━━━━━━━━━━━━ ✐ ━━━━━━━━━━━━━━

THE MESSAGES
OF THE MOMENT

The sky becomes overcast and the sound of distant thunder heralds the arrival of a welcome summer rain. Moving quickly, people in town take in their parked bicycles, shutter their windows, and grab the jacket they left on a porch railing. The natural world delivers news of an impending shower. We learned long ago to respond and avoid getting wet.

We need not look far to see how we are constantly being given signs, cues and clues to steer us through life's journey. An unexpected encounter in an airport waiting room leads to a major career change. You have a question about your car and the phone rings. It is your cousin the auto mechanic. Or, injuring your ankle, you must pass up a show at the theater, and end up at home having a most enriching and important talk with your roommate. Just as sure as the fragrance of roses in the living room is linked to the large bouquet on the coffee table, we live in an interconnected world of magic and message.

A mosaic of meaning, the occurrences of daily living reflect the active presence of the divine unity that is always here. From moment to moment, the proceedings of life are registered in the field of oneness, everything communicating with everything else. Returning to openness, alert to what our experience tells us, we begin to access the spiritual dimension at continuous play within the mystery of life. Leaving behind clinging to life's roller coaster of pleasure and discomfort, we instead embrace the larger picture, accepting that everything changes and exchanges according to a vast, incalculable cosmic dance. Our choices in life are inexorably bound to the greater scheme. Even our most horrendous difficulties are sent not to hurt us, not to punish, but to affirm and redefine our choices and needs. Gently informing us at times, life powerfully challenges us at others. Asked to meet that moment in a fresh way, we may be moved to examine and surmount even our greatest fears. Events are often sent as teachers, asking us to stretch or reverse our direction, reflect, reconsider and act from our present spiritual understanding.

Compassion and Belief

If you fall and scrape your knee, you can choose to see if there's a meaning or a message in your fall. We can learn to become increasingly open and skillful in this area of personal experience. It is a grave error, however, for someone other than ourselves to decide why something or another has happened to us. It is equally off-base for us to make that determination for someone else, unless they specifically ask for our opinion or help.

The role of a compassionate friend needs to be one of acceptance, not judgment or analysis. Finding the meaning in another's illness, injury, or life circumstance is not our job. The innate divine gift of human giving and compassion can be distorted by our own arrogance. It is not for us to judge another's suffering, only to empathize with it.

In recent years, there have been a number of popular books that assign certain spiritual meanings to specific illnesses. Some of them say, for example, that a cold means you are sad. Such books have helped many people in their sincere quest for enlarged meaning and healing. But they also have had a serious downside when they have been unwittingly abused to supplant natural human caring and loving with an abstract view of another person's suffering. Again, unless someone has discovered the meaning of an illness for himself, it is not compassionate to encourage abstract evaluations of the causes. These interpretations should be left to the individual. We cannot disrespect another's freedom. A belief, not an absolute truth, it is only a helpful view for those who discover and embrace it through serious personal search or inquiry. They must come to understanding in their own way and own timing. Our work is ultimately to learn compassion, not to lay prescribed points of dogma upon someone else's suffering. If we cannot restrain ourselves from thinking about what we believe may be messages in another's suffering, then we should at least remain silent. Staying present and sensitive to how one can honestly help would appear to be the path of harmlessness and goodwill.

Blame, guilt, and harsh fundamentalism breed from the dark shadows of truth twisted by imperfect human design. Rather than limiting beliefs to what is happening in one's own life, fundamental thinking uses belief as a weapon of its own ego to wield power and interfere with another's free will. It leads to controlling behavior and stifling choice, the antithesis of spiritual guidance. Imparting meaning and message, interpreting other people's experience is a dangerous and often false track. This error has less to do with spirit and more to do with power and control, and has been the bane of the honest human sacred impulse. It has given spirituality a bad name, emphasizing authority and power over inquiry, sensitive application of each person's free will, and overriding respect for individual choice.

Each of us must be free to believe what is spiritually viable for ourselves at any moment. We will then receive our measure of information in proportion to spiritual need. Otherwise, handing over expertise to others with their own beliefs and sometimes with their own agendas, we give up our own sacred resources and power. In general, with only the most rare exception, helpful impulses need to be well considered before we act upon them, for sometimes they can do more harm than good. We have plenty to deal with in our own spiritual journey without causing difficulties in someone else's.

Not by Chance

Lydia, an older woman, has been asked by a close colleague, thirty years her junior, if she would join her and her new boyfriend—just the three of them—for dinner. The young woman, Sarah, valuing Lydia's maturity and insight, wants her friend and coworker's opinion of this new man in her life. Lydia meets Sarah and her boyfriend in front of Sarah's apartment building, and they walk a couple of blocks to the restaurant. As they stroll, the man is in the middle, his arm around Sarah. They are in a separate world, making no effort to include Lydia as they walk. Lydia feels a gut sense that she is in the wrong place at the wrong time. She wonders why she was invited, since she is being isolated rather than included in this dinner engagement. At the restaurant this pattern continues, Lydia sitting opposite the two young lovers as they whisper in each other's ear and hold each other. Lydia feels like an intruder who mistakenly dropped into a couple's intimate time. Lydia feels she should go. She quickly devises a strategy to make a phone call and come back with news that there is an unexpected, pressing problem at home that she suddenly must attend to. But by now the food has been ordered, and she decides that she can't leave now. She eats her meal alone, apart and uncomfortable, occasionally feigning a polite smile. She tolerates this predicament, not wanting to step outside of familiar social amenities. Lydia has always been the good and tolerant one, and doesn't want to do or say anything that might break the charade taking place. At the end of the meal, she is asked to pay her share of the bill. The couple takes leave of Lydia at the restaurant exit. Lydia walks back to her car, alone, feeling relieved to get away from this rather selfish behavior. As she moves within six feet of her car, a taxi bashes into her left fender and a bit of the side. The car has to be towed away, and Lydia spends thirty-five dollars on a taxi ride home.

At the time of the experience, Lydia had not been exposed to a way of accepting the knocks of life as messages. She took it quite in the usual way: It was a bad day, her colleague Sarah and her boyfriend were unbearably selfish and childish, and the cab driver should never have been given a license. It was the kind of day she should have stayed in bed.

A few years later, however, Lydia had a shift in her world view. She became less bound exclusively by mechanistic thinking. Now validating her intuitive gifts, she wholeheartedly embraced the spiritual dimensions of her life. She began to see the way things worked beyond solely material forces. Sensing herself as part of something larger, an intelligent universal order was at times as obvious to her as would be a dialogue with an inseparable friend.

The message she had received that evening, she believes, was an attempt by a compassionate universe to get her to end enslavement and inertia, to advocate and act on behalf of her own basic well-being. Recalling the incident, she remembers how her gut and heart had literally told her the direction to take. Her gut had told her something was amiss, and her heart told her what to do about it. Her quickest path was presented to her as a clear communiqué to leave the restaurant. This, she feels, was the plainly evident message at the time, meant to move her beyond addictive clinging to "not rocking the boat" and conventional politeness at all costs, to act from a point of courage and compassion, even if the compassion was for her own self. She had always been overly kind and accommodating. Conditioned this way, to the exclusion of other possibilities, it wasn't the first time she had sacrificed her most basic ability to reasonably respond to a visceral imperative and had to eat the consequences.

These gut feelings are unquestionably physical experiences, resonating in the corresponding part of our organism. Not mere "passing thoughts," these signs of truth in a message or situation are registered on an energetic, electrical level and translated into actual physiological sensations. They feel as substantial as a headache or a good laugh. They are, however, often quite subtle, and require interest and observation before we become familiar with their unique insistence in our daily experience. It is simply a matter of practice and faith that they are an important access point for spiritual knowing.

Lydia saw that she had been told a direction but turned it down. Instead of acting, she had listened to secondary thoughts like, "It is too late, the food is here." These mental sidetracks camouflaged the simple trail and she once again was lost in a field of thorns. The divine force is persistent, and Lydia feels she was being shown by her discomfort that she had denied her inner sacred compass. But at the time it was happening, she still hadn't gotten the message. She believes the universe sent her the further isolation of walking to her car unescorted that night, to tell her that she needs to walk on her own and not concern herself unduly with the opinions of others. Eventually, the taxi "accident," like the vigorous crash of sacred cymbals, appeared as the most shocking alarm. But Lydia feels it was not an accident at all, but a clear-cut, well-designed message embodying a simple principle: If the initial divine message isn't heard and heeded, the volume is eventually turned up until we awaken and act in accord with the truer self. The taxi ride home Lydia saw as a finishing summation, like the last segment of a chapter in an epic novel, reasserting in distilled form a previously implied idea: "It is telling me that I need to act upon what is being told by the universe. The ride home told me I am spending too much of myself hanging on to an unhealthy way of being. I need to discard parts of myself that are no longer beneficial. It is a sacrifice a lot more profound than the thirty-five dollar message."

Divine Intention

What we believe is the basis of our possibility. How we act in relation to those beliefs is basic to the unfolding of our life. Having a pure belief that you will enter the profession of photography, you take the necessary steps to do so. Two years later, you find yourself a busy freelance photographer, doing head shots for actors and performers and an occasional journalism assignment.

This is not an accident, but a result of the creative process at work in everything we behold. A large proportion of our experience with life springs from the seeds of our personal belief. Some beliefs are helpful and others are obstacles. By reading the messages, we get a clue to the beliefs we live by.

Fran and Allen were two highly gifted, creative people. Fran, a teacher of movement and a gifted counselor, and Allen, a talented healer and massage therapist, loved their work dearly but feared they would never have a significant amount of material wealth in their lives. They came up with a clever scheme to create a novelty item that they would sell by mail order. They took all the necessary steps, finding manufacturers, purchasing stock and placing an expensive test advertisement in a major publication. There were lawyers' fees, incorporation fees, and storage rent to pay.

The day the advertisement came out, the stock market dropped: It was the famous market "adjustment" of October 1987, precipitating a severe recession and a decline in sales of unnecessary goods and services. Almost no orders came in.

Rather than taking it as a challenge to make their business work, regroup and try again in a different way, they immediately lost steam, felt defeated, and only applied the most minimal effort to recuperate their financial losses. Exhibiting none of the passion and recoil that is the hallmark of true business people, they feared spending more of their hard-earned money, taking more risk and plunging into the unknown. The venture collapsed into disarray.

Soon after it all went under, they were discussing the event very frankly. They realized that they were never truly interested in making lots of money, but they were interested in helping people. They had gone against a deep commitment in themselves to do what they felt was their passion and work on this earth. Falsely believing that they could be entrepreneurs, they had denied what they knew in their heart, mind, and guts. Business as a profession was not their way in the world, but teaching and healing was.

Fran and Allen both grew into models for their profession and are now even much more well off financially, earning adequate fees from many of their clients, doing what they love to do. Rather than letting a defeat create a negative void in their life, they chose to read the message of their own behavior and the events surrounding it to uncover what they truly believed. It had taken but a moment of reflection over dinner to transform an apparent disaster and personal disappointment into a major turn toward what was truly in line with their beliefs. They needed the "hard knock" to wake them up to what lay covered over by unexamined fear. They became much more trusting of their movements in life, and now listen carefully to what life is telling them moment to moment.

There are those who, professionally wedded to pure scientific inquiry, are now assuming an underlying interconnectedness and intelligence to all phenomena. Choosing to accept our part in this unity, there exists nothing independent. Isolated events simply don't happen. There is no such thing as being separate from this oneness. Having faith that a unity pervades, we acknowledge our own participation in the events that transpire in life. Entering into a courageous commitment to our belief, we wish to eliminate internal conflicts that come from actions and choices at odds with a deeper knowing. Evolving beyond a meaningless cycle of pleasure and pain, we shift into a spiritual perspective. Certainly life has joy and sorrow, but we are endowed with an inherent ability to take a transcendent leap into the unknown. When we not only swallow what life brings, but also digest it for a sacred purpose, the spiritual life receives nutrition and grows.

The birthday of your friend Sheila is on Friday. You call her, but by a slip of the tongue you inadvertently let her know that there is a surprise party planned in her honor. We say to another friend who planned the party, "I am sorry. That was not my intention when I called." You feel bad, but is there a message in the event? There was a discrepancy between your intention and your behavior, or at least the result of your behavior. The message might be waiting in the language of the apology to be discovered. Maybe it is something about being clear in your intentions with people, or perhaps a need to communicate more consciously when on the phone. It's also possible that the message is that you really didn't like the idea of it being a surprise and hadn't accepted that it would be. The possibilities are endless, but one needs to practice absolute honesty with oneself in order to touch the true and resonant places in us that know. Perhaps, unable to assign meaning to the message, you find out later that Sheila had a heart condition that might not have withstood the shock of a surprise.

So, unbeknownst to you, you were sent on a mission of mercy. Such things do happen. Honoring intuited feeling, a sympathetic resonance, a gut knowing, we are led in any direction to many life issues. This divine switchboard is continuously sending and receiving calls, letting us know that spirit pervades all life and that we are neither lost nor forgotten on our path.

The larger intention of the divine may hide in our daily events, encounters, and choices. Whether they be joyful or sorrowful, it is our privilege to ask for meaning. Sometimes the message is unfathomable, yet, even then, we are presented with a profound opportunity. Learning how to develop a purer trust in an intelligence far greater than our own is the task of a lifetime. We are often beckoned to know the joy of a healthy humility in the presence of an eternal, unknowable "now." For we also were not meant to know everything going on in the universe. Engaged in an active dialogue with an unseen reality, we stay awake and alert. Asking, we are also open to the unpredictable mysteries of our conversation with the divine source, not knowing what answers may (or may not) be given.

The Merciful Mirror

There are times when things just seem to fall miraculously into place. Stretching out a welcoming carpet, the universe leads us down a path of least resistance. This fluency of occurrence often happens when our desire for something is strong and deep, when it has become part of what we dream of day and night. There is a well-known saying, Be careful of what you wish for, because you just might get it. Understanding this principle, it becomes incumbent upon us to watch carefully, to monitor our wants so that they are in accord with our deepest purpose. Life is given to us to weigh our wants and choices so that they are continuously realigned with our moral imperative, our deepest sense of the right thing to do.

Maintaining a path absolutely coordinated by our sacred impulse is highly unlikely. But the circumstances and events of our life serve as a mirror to more adequately see and know ourselves, providing focus and direction from outer events as needed. Strong hints telling us to pay attention or correct an error show up with an unmistakable impact. For example, we may find ourselves getting angry at the world, feeling that people lack generosity. Those coming into our life lately may seem decidedly stingy and lack the natural giving impulse. We feel hurt and a bit perplexed. We are entitled to ask, Why is this happening to me and what is it telling me? Is there some stinginess in myself that the universe is telling me about? Is it due to a false self-image, believing I am generous when I know I give in order to get? Am I being pushed to look at the nature of generosity? Do I relate to other people with an eye on their contribution to my life, or do I meet them with no agenda?

There exists a universal spiritual principle stating that the world mirrors back to us that which we need to work on in ourselves. Events happen, but it is not by chance that we are there at that moment. It is ours to discover the message that may be there for us to grow. By asking the questions, we often find some very surprising truths surfacing that are all for the good. Not about divine retribution, but rather, a form of mercy, we can trust that there is a beneficent hand at work in the whole story. We are being given a chance to examine ourselves in a way that may never have occurred without the poignant mirror of the phenomenal world. It is a means to help us move closer to our spirit, access more clarity, and make a turn in our lives for the better. These reflected issues and events can be seen as the insistence of the divine to purify us as we walk our path, to cleanse our life of that which goes against the whispering but knowing deeper self. The messages are consistently right there, but the choice is always ours to receive them. Once we feel the validity of a message, we can directly change our belief and behavior and then move on.

The World Within Us

Turning on the nightly news, we see the ravages of war, the ghostly figures of starving children, urban blight, poverty, injustices, family violence, street killings, senseless slaughter and every conceivable version of destructive madness. Picking up the newspaper, we read of the death of the oceans, the depletion of oxygen levels, ozone holes and toxic residues of industrialization poisoning every corner of our planet.

One person responds to the message as a call to social action, another to a career in urban planning. A painter decides she needs to run an art auction to help an environmental advocacy organization fight the creation of a new coal strip mine, a retired teacher helps tutor homeless inner city children, and a businessman begins a program to help an economically disadvantaged village get out of the cycle of poverty. Each one acts according to his own particular sense of urgency. There are times when an entire community comes together because a message appears so obvious and so strong that the human spirit is compelled to act from the deepest recesses of its divine origin.

Some people who have been thrust into rescue work after a major disaster have reported being changed forever. The unexpected disaster happened and they were "called" into selfless service, the interconnected web of life urging them on to help others to live. Life, death, moral duty, fate, and the wish to serve beyond the self became as real and tangible as the crushing wounds of the hundreds under the rubble they were digging through.

Faced with a concrete need, we act in the world on behalf of the good. Taking in the images that shock or alarm us, we also have the opportunity to examine our own inner condition. The choices we are making in our own life are contributing to the state of the world. The problems in the world are a collective reflection of the problems going on inside of the individual inhabitants of the world. What happens to one is happening to us all. It is an indivisible tapestry made up of singular threads in an intricate weave.

When we see the violence in the world, do we ever question the vestiges of violence we carry in our own life? Do we take the image inside and say to ourselves: I am a part of the world. Am I without rage or hostility, undisturbed, free of conflict? Am I at war with someone or myself?

When we behold the greed of a corporation that puts profits and materialism before human life, do we reflect on our own avarice that blinds itself to other factors? Seeing people on TV in advanced starvation, we sit undecided about which restaurant to go to. Can we embrace that contradiction, question a habit like overeating? Am I making any personal effort to live not polluting the environment? Do I have to use the car and make more exhaust or can I do without milk for one meal? These are all questions that one can raise in the face of the images and stories we meet each day in the media to correct our portion of Creation even in a small way. Willing to feel the discomfort of honest self-examination, we discover a precious access point for human and planetary renewal.

Could it be that the media exist now at such a degree of efficiency and availability to so much of the Earth precisely in order to make us feel this connection to ourselves and our interconnections with each other? Perhaps television images and the World Wide Web are a serious divine message for the planet. We may be compelled to open the envelope and read the letter for ourselves and for the well-being of the whole world. Time may be running out.

Conclusion

THE COLORS OF LIFE

There is nothing stingy about Creation. Human existence is diversity itself, composed of all types of people with individual predilections, beliefs, and experiences. The light of awareness is the inner beacon we carry to illuminate our being and reveal its sacredness and responsibilities. When this light dims, meaningless suffering ensues, leaving us lost in the thick forest of forgetting. Losing our way in the shadows, it is only occasional that we meet the stream that leads us to the open sunlit field of fulfillment. We aspire to follow that stream so that the rare, accidental encounter with spirit is replaced by an honest, purposeful pursuit.

Daily, dawn teaches us how light differentiates into variety. When the unified rays of the sun meet the retreating darkness on the horizon, they give birth to the miracle of color and variation that reminds us of the nature of existence. It is the infiltration of the rising morning sunlight into the shaded obscurity of the landscape producing the explosion of color that has been the perennial inspiration of artists, poets and saints. While we may not be an artist, a poet or a saint by profession, we are all blessed with our own form of artistry, our own poetic expression and

107

our own wish to serve the greater good. Though our circum-stances are, by definition, our select experience, the quality, direc-tion, and transformation of that experience is largely up to us.

The options that presented to the contemporary human spirit may be more accessible and diversified today—and cer-tainly more available in book form. But these formulations con-tain recurrent sacred themes, resounding and restating themselves through millennia of recorded history, passing by way of the dimension of time into the timeless dimension of the moment.

A motivated college student working part-time to make ends meet is pushed onward by the loving hand of a childhood wish to be a doctor and help heal the sick. A writer working on a mag-azine article at home finds a moment of physical presence by preparing her tea with the conscious awareness and poise, as if in quiet ceremony and gratitude to the gift of life. A parent watches her firstborn dancing in glee in a playground and, through her quiet work with her attention, comes to touch the liv-ing feeling of generation continuity and divine plan. An active businessman catches himself rushing needlessly, and consciously slows down his stride so that he can come back to his senses and "smell the roses." He holds the elevator for a stranger, going against his usual habit of ignoring anyone else around him. All are reflections of the spirit, reaching beyond the constraints of time into the source of human possibility and meaning.

People can be radically different in their talents and tastes. As we can clearly notice in the workplace, some relate more to action and physicality, others to thinking. Some live more intu-itively, others more logically. Some consider a project, others feel it. One is not better than the other, any more than the blues and greens of a successful painting are better than the red-orange hues. Each has its strengths and ways, contributing its part to the global picture and the colors of life.

We are well aware that it is not beyond us to trouble the mind about something that can be easily reconciled by taking action. Beholding a vista of myriad options of spiritual practice, we may fail to act decisively. Inspired by words but then doing nothing about it wreaks havoc on the spirit. Time and time again the impulse to act can be lost to procrastination and inertia. This is self-defeating to the spirit and makes further growth difficult. Denigrating to the human will, it creates inner conflict through the denial of our deepest yearnings. Choosing, however, one sacred practice, clearly identified, and doing it for a significant amount of time, we derive the benefits that come with repetition and consistency. Like softly blowing on an ember to ignite a bigger flame, we then follow a course of experiential learning as we would in developing any skill.

There are distinct advantages to following a specific practice for a goodly amount of time. If we are sincere in our interest, it behooves us to cut through the confusion, wishful thinking and mental speculation and to undertake a sincere study of real importance. As in learning to run long distances, it is most productive to start out small. There is no rush to accomplishment, no goal orientation, in honest spiritually motivated activity. It can involve simply pausing for a second before opening doors, to confront the unconscious condition that rules our mechanicality. Practicing an awareness of kindness and generosity when you shop, listening to your dreams, or tying your shoe with an added interest in being with the whole gesture is as valid and valuable as other suggested possibilities. Using any idea presented in this book or from another source, we can be creative. There exists no rote formula but rather a sense of well-directed practicality extending our attention toward the sacred that we want to serve. Some will improvise a study that conforms with their unique lifestyle or situation. The essential elements are intention and awareness, regardless of the activity pursued. But taking it on, whatever "it" may be, is the only step that truly works.

While it is true that personal benefits need not be underestimated for what they add to our own well-being and happiness, the consciousness we contribute to a moment is an offering to all of Creation. There is a responsibility that comes with being human that is larger than any self-help we may undertake.

Much depends on how we see our mission and where we are in our own lives. We need to work on our own spiritual development, starting with ourselves and where we are. There is no escaping this fact. It has been the experience of the world that the more evolved the helper, the more evolved the help. But we would be foolhardy to lose sight of the sacred imperative of human relations and societal concerns in order to grow personally. From a spiritual standpoint, there is simply no such thing as self-help. Rather, there are the efforts we make on behalf of Creation that contribute to the good of all. Since we are part of the whole, we therefore need to help ourselves and take care of the immediate parcel we received on loan for a lifetime. If that means we need more focus, attentiveness, purposefulness, open heartedness, presence, and self-knowledge of our inner world, in order to do our share in the creative cycle of evolution, then we have connected to an honest spiritual need. If our need is unrelated to a sense of gratitude for and service to life itself, it cannot with integrity be labeled particularly healthful food for the spirit. Rather, then, it is self-interest, not spiritual necessity that is the leading edge of an action. This, then, remains a function of ego, until the impulse to improve something in ourselves is elevated to include a larger wish for the well-being of everything existing. If there is a goal to spiritual practice it is to illuminate our being with a point of view helpful to all life and in service to a greater order.